| srat richtsrat ihtsrat | Obermusikmeister 2 Sterne: Stabsmusikmeister ohne Stern: Musikmeister | Hauptmann d. R. (Nachr.-Truppe) (graue Tuchunterlage) | Hauptmann d. Landw. (Inf.) (graue Tuchunterlage) | Stabszahlmeister 1 Stern: Oberzahlmeister ohne Stern: a. p. Zahlmeister |

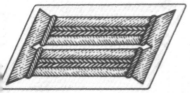

Übrige Offiziere

KRAGENPATTEN
MIT STICKEREIEN
ZUM WAFFENROCK

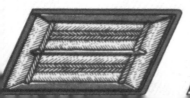

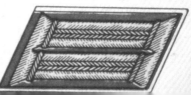

ALLIED INTELLIGENCE

HANDBOOK TO THE
GERMAN ARMY 1939–45

**COMPILED AND INTRODUCED
BY STEPHEN BULL**

CONWAY

BLOOMSBURY

LONDON · OXFORD · NEW YORK · NEW DELHI · SYDNEY

Conway
An imprint of Bloomsbury Publishing Plc

50 Bedford Square
London
WC1B 3DP
UK

1385 Broadway
New York
NY 10018
USA

www.bloomsbury.com

CONWAY and the 'C' logo are trademarks of Bloomsbury Publishing Plc

First published 2017

© Stephen Bull, 2017

British Library Cataloguing-in-Publication Data
A catalogue record for this book is available from the British Library.

Library of Congress Cataloguing-in-Publication data has been applied for.

ISBN: HB: 978-1-8448-6426-3
ePDF: 978-1-8448-6428-7
ePub: 978-1-8448-6429-4

2 4 6 8 10 9 7 5 3 1

Typeset in Bulmer MT by Deanta Global Publishing Services, Chennai, India
Printed and bound in Great Britain by CPI Group (UK) Ltd, Croydon, CR0 4YY

MIX
Paper from
responsible sources
FSC® C020471

To find out more about our authors and books visit www.bloomsbury.com. Here you will find extracts,
author interviews, details of forthcoming events and the option to sign up for our newsletters.

Contents

Introduction

There have been many descriptions of the German Army in the Second World War: most published since 1945 with the benefit of hindsight and often little idea of how information was gathered. This obscures the crucial point that during the conflict obtaining up-to-date material on the enemy was extremely difficult, while producing authoritative documents for use by British and US forces was a potential matter of life or death. A wary enemy kept as much as possible secret, and in a fast-moving war what was accurate today was frequently out of date by the time it had been published in a form accessible to the fighting soldier. This cycle of collection, analysis, processing and dissemination might take months, and sifting the wheat from the chaff was as much an art form as a science. As a result the 'fog of war' applied just as readily to military intelligence as it did to the battlefield, and manuals and bulletins flowed thick and fast in an effort to keep up.

What is attempted here is a snapshot of the work of intelligence, as well as of its target. For if the German Army was dynamic, moving and developing from campaign to campaign, so also was its shadow, the series of time lag images produced by those who sought to capture its character, strength and collective state of mind. What is replicated in the following chapters is not therefore just one intelligence manual of the German Army, but a collection from different publications, both US and British, created over the course of the war, plus a sample of the source documents and illustrations with which intelligence officers had to work. Some of the pictures painted by the Allies were full, detailed and pretty accurate; others sketchy and episodic, occasionally coloured by preconceptions or a desire not to leave a daunting impression of technical excellence or cause the discouragement of the reader.

British General Staff Handbooks of the German Army, first produced well before 1914, were revised during the First World War and supplemented by many different types of manual and, from 1917, the complementary output of the US War Department, which had German documents translated and edited at its Army War College. By the end of the First World War the US 'Military Intelligence Division' alone numbered more than 1,500 personnel, officers, agents and civilian staff. 'Intelligence officers' were also attached to military units in the field, down to battalion level.

Sadly much was unlearned in the inter-war period, and by 1936 the US Military Intelligence Division numbered fewer than 70 people. Despite subsequent expansion of the various intelligence organisations the success of the Signal Intelligence Service in cracking the codes of the Japanese 'Purple' cipher machine in 1940 was not replicated in efforts aimed at Germany. Initially the British had scarcely better fortune. In 1936 a 'Z' organisation for running agents in Germany and Italy was formed under Claude Dansey at Bush House on the Strand. Agents were dispatched to '12-Land', their code for Germany, and at least a handful of anti-Nazi Germans were 'turned' to work for the UK. One young British officer, under cover of working for a film company, toured Austria and Germany with the brief of creating an 'Order of Battle'. Yet overall impact was limited, as were the efforts of personnel embedded in embassies, overwhelmed by work which included processing passports for would-be émigrés.

From September 1939 Britain was at war with Germany. The US, which was not, maintained a diplomatic presence; moreover, American journalists retained freedom to report from inside the Third Reich. Some of these reporters were of German ancestry and fluent German speakers. In one remarkable example Louis P Lochner accompanied German forces during the invasion of the Low Countries and France, returning ambivalent copy juxtaposing reports of sentimental child-friendly German soldiery with the burning of Louvain library and all the horrors of 'modernest' [*sic*] warfare. With the outbreak of war between the US and Germany in December 1941, Lochner and 137 other newsmen were interned at Bad Nauheim, but were repatriated five months later.

The establishment of the Secret Intelligence Service communications 'war station' at Bletchley Park early in 1939, good relations with Czechoslovak and Polish intelligence, relocation of 'Z' to Switzerland and the formation of the Special Operations Executive (SOE) all gradually improved British military intelligence gathering. In early 1940 a team including Alan Turing, working under Alfred Knox, built on earlier Polish efforts to crack the 'Green' key of the German Army Enigma code. Later the same year Britain and the US moved towards full exchange of cryptographic information, and in America 'Wild Bill' Donovan was promoted 'COI' or 'co-ordinator' of all forms of intelligence, and subsequently to head the Office of Strategic Services (OSS). Despite rivalries, significant amounts of information were shared, not least about German forces and their dispositions.

DIAGRAM F

GERMAN
PARACHUTIST,
SHOWING
TYPICAL
UNIFORM AND
HARNESS

A rough sketch of a German parachutist from *Home Guard: A Handbook
for the LDV*, 1940. Early expectations were that Local Defence Volunteers
would confront enemy airborne troops, but these patriots had a nasty habit of shooting
at anybody dangling from a parachute. As a result illustrations like this, and
instructions to open fire only when the number of
jumpers exceeded the number of men in a bomber crew,
were issued in mainly to save British pilots.

In 1942 the US Military Intelligence Division reorganised so that it no longer
performed operational functions, but acted as planning and policy maker, co-
ordinating the efforts of the US Army and Navy. The US Army itself now
fielded three intelligence organisations: the Military Intelligence Service, the
Signal Security Agency and the Counter Intelligence Corps. From March 1942
the Military Intelligence Service was tasked with the production of intelligence
on the Germans for use by front line commanders. The organisation was then
headed by Brigadier-General Hayes Kroner, who had served in London as a

military attaché during 1934 to 1938, as observer in England early in 1941 and with the 'British Empire' section of the Intelligence Branch.

While operational intelligence on the German Army was gathered through a variety of means including decryption, espionage, battlefield observation and aerial photography, a surprising volume of material was obtained by far less dramatic means. Conflict zones were scoured for equipment, and prime items such as new tanks, guns and shells were hauled off to specialist facilities to be painstakingly disassembled, analysed, tested, measured, weighed, photographed and reassembled, then tested again, sometimes to destruction. Prisoners were also an important source of information, but there was much

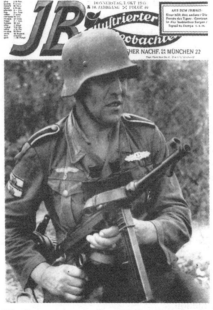

Open publications were scoured by Allied intelligence and enemy propaganda was replete with photos like this example from a 1943 periodical, showing a German soldier armed with an MP 40 sub-machine gun wearing 'tank destruction' arm badges. Problems arose when the enemy issued images of rare or fanciful items or exaggerated specifications.

more to extracting material than interrogation, with or without bribes or threats.

Even before the Second World War started, a British 'Combined Services Detailed Interrogation Centre' to deal with selected enemy prisoners was planned. After a modest start at the Tower of London this was formally established in December 1939 at Trent Park near Barnet, with further 'Distribution Centres' brought into use in 1942, at Latimer House and Wilton Park in Buckinghamshire. Useful subjects for the process included high-ranking officers and anybody familiar with the latest technology and weapons. To facilitate triage of enemy prisoners a 'Prisoner of War Interrogation Section (Home)' was formed during 1940, and new prisoners were sorted in various holding 'cages' on arrival in the UK. British effort with enemy prisoners fell ultimately under the direction of MI19, which also had responsibility for assisting the escape of British prisoners. In 1945 Operation Epsilon established another centre, for German nuclear scientists, at Farm Hall.

The US decided to adopt similar methods in 1941, and by 1942 the first two American centres, jointly run by the US Army and Navy, were in business. The most important of these was at Fort Hunt. As of 1943, it was agreed that all specially selected prisoners should be available to both US and UK intelligence. In the run-up to the invasion of Europe in 1944 additional facilities were established for sifting UK and US prisoners at Kempton Park and Devizes respectively.

Surreptitious recording of prisoners in 'M' ('microphoned') rooms was crucial. Arguably this was most effective at Trent Park where a staff of more than a hundred, many of them anti-Nazi Germans and Austrians, many with Jewish backgrounds, was engaged in listening. As there was no continuous recording facility the eavesdroppers had to turn on a machine and cut a disk when interesting conversations developed. Discussion was stimulated by housing prisoners from different units of the same rank together, and by introducing 'stool pigeons' into the special camps to raise specific subjects or provoke interaction.

Remarkably, the enemy gained a fair idea of what was going on after prisoner exchanges and the escape of Franz von Werra in 1941, but warnings issued to German personnel about keeping their mouths shut were largely ineffective. By the end of the war more than 300 German generals and a multitude of other staff officers and personnel had passed through the bugged rooms. When Allied

INDIVIDUAL TRAINING

A mountain trooper on skis throwing a grenade, from the US Military
Intelligence Special Series manual no. 20, *German Ski Training and Tactics*,
1943. This was an edited translation of a German manual with redrawn
images. Standard issue of such booklets was 150 copies per US division.

forces entered Germany itself a fresh wave of intelligence gathering took place
with the tracking down of key personnel and the examination and dismantling
of research facilities and factories.

Such exotic methods could bear remarkable fruit, but a significant quantity
of material was also drawn from what are now called 'open source' means.
Consulting an open source might be as simple as ordering a foreign textbook or
manual, or walking into a library in a neutral country and browsing newspapers.
Sometimes it might be the study of images in enemy propaganda or pictures
taken by German Army photographers on campaign. Useful illustrated stories
and reports appeared both in publications within the Reich and in the pages
of propaganda organs such as *Signal*, a fortnightly magazine printed in many
different languages, including English, which reached a peak circulation of two
and a half million copies.

Informing the Allied serviceman about the German Army completed the
circle. Booklets were the obvious method, but it was realised that variety and
an entertainment element gave the best chance lessons would be learned.
Films, lectures, handling enemy equipment and exercises featuring troops

portraying a German force were therefore added to the repertoire. The printed word itself also required constant refreshment and revision. So it was that manuals and bulletins appeared in series, such as the British *Periodical Notes on the German Army*, *Enemy Weapons*, the American *Technical and Tactical Trends* and the Military Intelligence Service *Intelligence Bulletin*. Sometimes updated information appeared as mere snippets within other documents such as the British *Army Training Memorandum* series or *Notes from Theatres of War*.

US military intelligence also produced an entire *Special Series* of short publications on subjects such as enemy tactics and equipment. As the series' preamble explained these were 'published for the purpose of providing officers with reasonably confirmed information from official and other reliable sources'. *German Tactical Doctrine* of December 1942, for example, was stated to be based on a 'partial resume of doctrine taught at the *Kriegsakademie*', which was itself largely a practical adaptation of the overarching German manual on command, the *Truppenführung*. *The German Squad in Combat*, 1944, was likewise a 'translation of the greater part of a German handbook' designed to aid squad training.

Some of the *Special Series* volumes were holistic in the sense that they combined information from a variety of enemy manuals, documents and other sources in an attempt to create a rounded picture of an entire subject. *German Mountain Warfare*, 1944, blended translated material from enemy manuals almost a decade old with new material, illustrations, organisational tables and information on equipment and tactics. Careful examination of its photographs shows that they were taken from diverse sources such as the German Army's own *Propagandakompagnie* and manuals, plus the British Army. Some other illustrations were redrawn by an artist engaged by the US Military Intelligence Service. As of early 1944, the *Special Series, Intelligence Bulletin* and *Tactical and Technical Trends* were the three major sources of information on the Germans for the US serviceman. All were distributed in the same manner as *Field Manuals* on American subjects. Current publications appeared in *FM 21-6 List of Publications for Training*.

Such unending and industrious intelligence activity, which lasted longer than the war itself, had significance far beyond the academic and mundane. For it tells us not just quite a lot about the German Army and its development, but about how Allied forces viewed their enemy, and what they actually knew about him at any given moment. Sometimes Allied intelligence got things

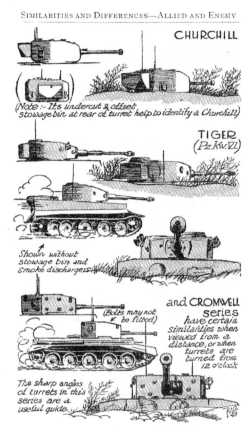

SIMILARITIES AND DIFFERENCES—ALLIED AND ENEMY

CHURCHILL

(Note:- Its undercut & offset
stowage bin at rear of turret help to identify a Churchill)

TIGER
(Pz.Kw.VI)

Shown without
stowage bin and
smoke dischargers.

and CROMWELL
series
have certain
similarities when
viewed from a
distance, or when
turrets are
turned from
12 o'clock

(Bolts may not
be fitted)

The sharp angles
of turrets in this
series are a
useful guide.

The practical application of intelligence: how the Tiger tank
can easily be distinguished from British armour. From
AFV Recognition, Amendment 1, 1944.

wrong or failed to update promptly; sometimes they chose to distribute one
piece of knowledge rather than another, and this was clearly of operational
import. Cumulatively it was also a war of the mind which modern histories
seldom visit.

Chapter 1

Periodical Notes on the German Army 1940

At about the outbreak of hostilities in 1939 the British War Office began a series of short publications entitled *Tactical and Technical Notes on the German Army*. During the early 'phoney war' period their focus was organisation and basic doctrine, since in the West there was little actual combat on which to report, although French and other foreign observations were taken into account. During 1940 practical experience of active operations rapidly accumulated, and it seems that the apparently static image presented by the existing title was no longer deemed adequate to sum up what was now a series of updates on an unpredictable enemy. The result was renaming and a symbolic fresh start with *Summary of Periodical Notes on the German Army No. 1*.

So it was that *Periodical Notes* became the British Army's prime method of keeping abreast of enemy developments, and progressively most aspects of the German Army were addressed. No. 16 covered the transport of troops by air; this information was brought abruptly up to date in 1941 with the attack on Crete, covered in issue 38. Issue 18, 'based on information received up to 1st May 1940', was the latest snapshot of the enemy on the very eve of the invasion of France and the Low Countries. This contained interesting passages, particularly on the tactics of German raiding parties, 'assault detachments' and the use of flame throwers – apparently gleaned from French reports – but no really compelling picture of how dramatically 'mobile troops' might operate.

Numbers 22, 23 and 27 of *Periodical Notes* covered the German signal service, infantry and artillery respectively. In February 1941 issue 35 had an especially strong tactical content, detailing training for close quarter fighting, orders and a longer piece on battle tactics destined to become part of the much bigger and more exhaustive volume *Notes on the German Army in War*. Issue 35 also contained a couple of items of a more propagandistic tone: one on 'German psychology' purportedly authored by 'an individual who was for many years resident in Germany', and another on the occupation of the Channel Islands. Issue 40 of June 1942 was particularly informative, being devoted to the 'Tactical Handling' of the German armoured division and statistics on its component parts.

Judging by a sample of the figures printed in the rear covers, *Periodical Notes* gradually increased its print run over time so that the 17,000 copies of June 1940 became 20,000 in October 1940, 30,000 in February 1941 and 50,000 by June 1942. The later editions of *Periodical Notes* were also slightly larger in format.

Our example, reproduced here in full, is issue 32 of September 1940. At this point, France, the Low Countries, Norway and Poland had all fallen to the German Army, and Britain was itself under threat of invasion. Issue 30 had already dealt with 'Lessons of the battle of France, and possible German tactics in an attack on Great Britain'. Issue 32 now filled in details of enemy reconnaissance units and general battle tactics.

The remarks on enemy morale, at the outbreak of war, during the phoney war and currently, are particularly fascinating. The 'Nazification' of German society was seen as playing no little part, and this was particularly relevant to the young who had little experience of living in any other form of state. 'Very high' morale was reinforced by victory, and only slightly tarnished by hardships such as rationing. Although the source is not quoted, the 'reliable' information that only 32 Germans had deserted in February 1941 and only 102 had overstayed leave out of an army of millions spoke volumes about the level of commitment of the ordinary soldier. According to British intelligence, there appeared to be generally good discipline and complete faith in the *Führer*, with only the possible exception of some troops posted far from home in the wilds of Norway or on the coasts of Western Europe.

PERIODICAL NOTES

ON THE

GERMAN ARMY

No. 32

Note: No. 31 of this series is a "Security" document

NOT TO BE TAKEN INTO THE FRONT LINE

Prepared by the
General Staff, The War Office

September, 1940

CONTENTS

A. RECONNAISSANCE UNITS IN THE GERMAN ARMY.
(From a German Manual.)

1. General.

Great demands are made on the commander and all the personnel of a reconnaissance unit. The personality of the commander is the deciding factor for success. Cunning, versatility, ability to grasp orders rapidly, determined driving or driving across any type of terrain, the offensive spirit, resourcefulness under all circumstances and especially at night, cold-bloodedness, and the ability to act quickly and independently, are all qualities which must be developed.

Orders to a reconnaissance unit must generally cover the following points:—

(*a*) Time of departure.

(*b*) Information about reconnaissance units on the flanks.

(*c*) Zones or general direction to be reconnoitred.

(*d*) Object of reconnaissance.

(*e*) Limits of reconnaissance.

(*f*) Arrangements for transmission of messages and for liaison with other reconnaissance units and/or reconnaissance aircraft.

(*g*) Line of advance and objective of main body.

(*h*) Information about the enemy and local inhabitants.

The higher commander issues orders regarding the liaison arrangements between air and ground reconnaissance and between motorized reconnaissance units and the reconnaissance units of infantry divisions.

2. Organisation and performance of reconnaissance units.

(*a*) The following is a guide for the composition of the motorized reconnaissance unit of an armoured division:—

> H.Q. and signals troop.
>
> Two armoured car squadrons.
>
> One M.C. squadron.
>
> One heavy squadron, consisting of:—
>
>> One 7·5 cm. (2·95 ins.) gun troop (motorized).
>>
>> One A.Tk. troop (motorized).
>>
>> One engineer troop (motorized).
>
> "A" echelon 1st line transport.

Ration echelon.

Light ammunition column.

"B" echelon 1st line transport (baggage).

(b) The following is a guide for the composition of the motorized reconnaissance unit of a motorized infantry division:—

H.Q. and signals troop.

One armoured car squadron.

One M.C. squadron.

"A" echelon 1st line transport.

Ration echelon.

Light ammunition column.

"B" echelon 1st line transport (baggage).

Motorized reconnaissance units can cover 120–160 miles in a day if there is no enemy resistance, ground conditions are favourable, and petrol supply assured.

The following are average rates of advance in the absence of enemy resistance:—

Motorized reconnaissance units approximately 18 m.p.h.

Armoured car troops approximately 25 m.p.h.

Darkness and mist considerably reduce these speeds.

An armoured car troop is capable of reconnoitring a zone 16 miles broad.

(c) The following is a guide for the composition of the partly motorized reconnaissance unit of an infantry division:—

H.Q. and signals troop.

One mounted squadron.

One cyclist squadron.

One heavy squadron, consisting of:—

One 7·5 cm. (2·95 ins.) gun troop.

One A.Tk. troop.

One armoured car troop.

"A" echelon 1st line transport.

Ammunition and stores echelon.

Ration echelon.

"B" echelon 1st line transport (baggage).

In the absence of enemy resistance and over favourable ground mounted and cyclist troops can cover approximately 45 miles in a day, armoured car troops approximately 160 miles, and the reconnaissance unit itself about 30–40 miles in a day.

The following may be taken as average rates of advance, in the absence of enemy resistance and over favourable ground:—

> Partly motorized reconnaissance unit: 4 m.p.h.
> Mounted troop: 5 m.p.h.
> Mounted orderlies: 6 m.p.h.
> Cyclist troop: 7–8 m.p.h.
> Armoured car troop: 25 m.p.h.

A squadron is generally capable of reconnoitring a zone 6 miles in width.

3. Tasks of reconnaissance units.

Superiority in the reconnaissance area facilitates our own reconnaissance and makes that of the enemy difficult; it also conceals movements of our own troops.

This superiority is gained by taking the offensive against the enemy's reconnaissance units and posts. It is, however, wrong for reconnaissance units to allow themselves to become involved in unnecessary engagements.

By taking advantage of its mobility, the reconnaissance unit may successfully engage even superior enemy forces. Its mobility frequently enables it to attack the flanks and rear of the enemy and achieve surprise, to deliver repeated attacks at different points, to concentrate its forces quickly to destroy small isolated enemy detachments, and to employ part of its strength as a mobile reserve or for counter-attacks in defence.

In the attack, a distinction must be drawn between an enemy strong point and an enemy defensive line. In the case of a strong point, the aim of the reconnaissance unit is to utilise its speed to surround and destroy the enemy. In the case of a defensive line, the aim is to concentrate all available forces and achieve a break-through at one point. It may not be advisable to reconnoitre suitable points for a break-through, if by so doing the intention to attack may be prematurely disclosed to the enemy. The reconnaissance unit will generally have to be reinforced, if it is to achieve a break-through in a strongly held defensive line.

In preparing an attack, orders as a rule will be issued first to the heavy weapons, so that the attack will not be delayed while the heavy weapons are preparing to come into action, and the element of surprise thus be lost. If an attack is held up, it may be advisable to break off the engagement and, taking advantage of the mobility of the reconnaissance unit, strike at another point. Reconnaissance units are particularly well adapted to pursue an enemy who has been forced to withdraw by the main force. If pursuit from a flank would mean loss of contact with the enemy owing to the distance being too great, the enemy should be pursued through the break-through.

A reconnaissance unit may be compelled by the task allotted to it or by enemy action temporarily to adopt the defensive. It can only defend itself successfully in ground which forces the enemy to attack on a narrow front, or alternatively its flanks must be protected by other troops. It is generally advisable to keep a mobile reserve to forestall enemy outflanking movements or for counter-attacks.

The reconnaissance unit is, however, more suited for delaying action than protracted defence.

4. Method of operation of motorized reconnaissance units.

Army reconnaissance units carry out strategic reconnaissance under the orders of the army to which they are allotted. Reconnaissance units of armoured and motorized infantry divisions carry out tactical reconnaissance under the orders of the divisions to which they are allotted.

The reconnaissance unit commander sends out patrols. Each patrol must, however, consist of at least two cars (including the W/T vehicle).

Patrols will be given lines, on crossing which they will report (by W/T or D.R., etc.) even if they have not been in contact with the enemy. Patrol commanders receive information verbally on the general situation (where contact with the enemy may be expected, and with what types of unit), ground, results of air and other reconnaissances, task allotted to the reconnaissance unit, and the commander's intentions.

The reconnaissance unit commander then issues orders verbally to the patrol commanders. Particular points on which reports are required should be given out in order of importance under the heading "I want to know".

A patrol should not as a rule be given more than one task. If demolitions are required, engineers should be attached to the patrol and move with it.

Reconnaissance at night is principally a question of watching roads and keeping the enemy under observation from woods and farms. Reconnaissance units should be relieved before first light, as it is not advisable to leave them in contact with the enemy for several days on end.

Reconnaissance units and patrols must be able to effect river crossings rapidly. Attacks on bridges on main roads are not as a rule likely to succeed. A feint attack may, however, be made on such bridges, while preparations are being made to cross at other undefended or less strongly defended points.

The engineers in a reconnaissance unit can carry out the following work:—

(*a*) Build a 5-ton bridge, 36 ft. long.
(*b*) Build and man two 2-ton rafts or one 4-ton raft.
(*c*) Build a foot-bridge for cyclists.

The commander of the reconnaissance unit decides whether to send the whole reconnaissance unit across or only the patrols. In the latter case the crossing point must as a rule be defended until the patrols return.

5. Method of operation of partly motorized reconnaissance units.

The partly motorized reconnaissance unit carries out tactical reconnaissance for an infantry division.

It should receive orders in good time so that it can get a sufficient start on the main body.

In country where immediate contact with the enemy is to be expected, the reconnaissance unit commander will divide the area to be reconnoitred into bounds. The patrols will be informed of the route on which the reconnaissance unit will advance. The bounds for the mounted and cyclist patrols should not as a rule be more than 10 miles in advance of the main body of the reconnaissance unit, unless W/T is available. The mounted orderlies and D.Rs. can then be sent back to it as they will know its bounds.

Mounted patrols are not dependent on roads, and can swim their horses across streams. They can search a sector in open order. They are not dependent on ground, weather, and not usually on supplies. Their rate of march and performance are limited.

Cyclist patrols in districts with good road systems and in favourable weather have a higher rate of march and a greater performance than mounted patrols. Their rate of march is however reduced on paths, particularly in bad weather. Across country their rate of advance may frequently be less than that of a man on foot. At night, provided there is a good road system, cyclist patrols are more suitable because of their noiselessness.

The armoured car patrol has a high rate of advance and performance. Its armour gives it superiority if unarmoured patrols are encountered, and as it is allotted a W/T vehicle, it can pass information back more quickly than other patrols. It is suitable for employment on roads and to cover great distances. It can carry out one task quickly and be available shortly afterwards to undertake another.

The strength of patrols of all types depends on their task, the ground, enemy dispositions and the attitude of the civil population. The strength of mounted patrols varies from a section to a troop. Cyclist patrols should generally be a troop strong, as being mainly confined to roads they have to fight for information more frequently than mounted patrols. The strength of an armoured car patrol must always be at least two cars (including the W/T car). Portable W/T sets may be allotted to the most important patrols. It must be borne in mind, however, that if wireless traffic is reduced to the minimum, it is more difficult for the enemy listening posts to discover the presence and movements of the reconnaissance unit.

As a rule patrols can work only by day. At night their activities will generally be limited to gaining and maintaining contact with the enemy and locating his foremost posts.

The reconnaissance unit is made up of elements which move at different speeds. The aim must be, in spite of these differences, to bring the mounted and cyclist squadrons forward in such a way that on contact with the enemy unified command of the reconnaissance unit is possible. If the situation requires it, the commander of the reconnaissance unit must not hesitate to push on with the mounted squadron, if the country is impassable for motor vehicles. Separation from the W/T sets and the necessity of relying entirely on mounted orderlies and D.Rs. for the transmission of messages must be reckoned with.

Mounted men, cyclists and motor-cyclists can cross streams rapidly in pneumatic boats. The reconnaissance unit has two large and two small pneumatic boats in the engineer stores wagon of the ammunition and stores echelon. These boats are manned by the engineers in the mounted and cyclist squadrons.

6. Gas contamination.

Patrol commanders should be trained and equipped for gas detection duties. The bulk of the gas detection personnel should generally be kept together with the reconnaissance unit. They reconnoitre the extent of contamination after the patrols have reported the existence of contaminated ground. The aim must be to get through a contaminated area quickly in order to gain information about the enemy's dispositions behind it. Armoured cars are particularly suitable for this purpose.

The removal of lightly contaminated obstacles which are holding up the motorized patrols is in the main a matter for the engineers allotted to reconnaissance units.

B. TACTICS OF GERMAN INFANTRY AND ITS SUPPORT BY OTHER ARMS.
(From a German Manual.)

Note by the General Staff.—This article was published in "Periodical Notes on the German Army No. 28" in shortened form. It is now considered to be of sufficient interest to be published again *in toto.*

1. The task of the infantry.
The infantry is the principal arm, and all other arms support it.

By fire and movement infantry defeats the enemy. Infantry breaks down the enemy's last resistance in the attack, and in the defence it holds out against his assault. The infantry carries the main weight of battle and suffers the heaviest losses. The effectiveness of infantry depends on its offensive spirit. This spirit, which depends on confidence in one's own arms, must be cultivated. Infantry tactics must be dominated by the will to advance and attack.

2. Infantry tactics.
Infantry tactics both in the attack and in the defence are based on fire. Even in hand-to-hand fighting the result is speedily decided by a bullet or hand-grenade.

The object of infantry fire in battle is to establish fire superiority, and so to overwhelm and destroy the enemy. It is the duty of infantry commanders to bring about this fire superiority by employing an appropriate number of weapons with sufficient quantities of ammunition, and by systematic fire control both as regards time and place.

In the attack all fire, in particular the concentrated fire of light and heavy weapons and artillery fire, must be exploited by infantry by rapid movements forward.

The most important part of all infantry training, from individual training to regimental training, is the use of fire. Mastery of the use of each weapon,

'An assault trooper from the battle at Verdun': a German Army
Propagandakompanie ('propaganda company') image released to the press in
June 1940. The soldier carries an MG 34 machine gun and holstered pistol.

the co-operation of all infantry weapons, their co-operation with artillery in
the attack, and the firm determination of each infantry soldier to utilise all fire
support to get on, and above all to help the advance by his own fire, are the
principles of this training.

The success of any attack depends on the offensive spirit of the infantry.
Troops, pressing forward to the fullest possible extent, must take full advantage
of all neutralisation of the enemy's fire, and in general of all fire directed against
the enemy.

In the assault all arms develop their maximum fire power. The accompanying
L.M.Gs. advance to within a very short distance of the enemy, firing at the enemy
immediately in front of them. Hand-grenades are used to deal with enemy under
cover. Armed with machine-pistols or rifles, platoon and section commanders
lead their men forward. The enemy, if still resisting, is overpowered in hand-
to-hand fighting. All the weapons in the forward zone which are not engaging
the point attacked bring fire to bear on the rear of the enemy's positions, or on

the flanks, if they are holding up the assaulting troops. Battalion and company commanders place themselves during the assault at key positions.

Artillery F.O.Os. accompany the infantry in the assault. Some of the artillery sections prepare to move to their forward positions.

3. Co-operation with the artillery.

Good liaison between infantry and artillery is of first importance.

It is facilitated:—

(*a*) When the two commanders try to site their H.Q. in such a way that personal contact is possible.

(*b*) When the O.Ps. and the gun positions are immediately behind the infantry which they are to support.

(*c*) When signal communications have been established.

The light and heavy artillery batteries make use of their liaison detachments to maintain close contact with the infantry. The liaison detachment of an artillery battery is usually sent by the battery commander to the point where artillery support is of the greatest importance and where direct observation can be of the greatest use in enabling the artillery to intervene rapidly. The liaison detachment is usually attached to the battalion which is to deliver the main thrust or which in the defence is to hold the position where the heaviest enemy attack is expected.

Co-operation between infantry and artillery is also facilitated by direct contact between the advanced elements of the infantry and the artillery O.Ps. and F.O.Os. Arrangements must be made in good time for artillery F.O.Os. to be attached to all the attacking battalions.

The position of O.Ps. must be known to all units. Infantry commanders and the F.O.Os. for the heavy infantry weapons must establish and maintain contact with the artillery F.O.Os. in their sector so as to co-ordinate observation and reconnaissance and requests for fire support. Conversely artillery F.O.Os. must maintain constant touch with the infantry in their vicinity.

4. System of plotting reference points.

In order that targets may be rapidly indicated and fire from all weapons concentrated on certain sectors of the ground, important points are noted as reference points.

The infantry reference points are described by the letter "I" followed by a number. These are known as "I points." The "I points" for use of a battalion are numbered from 100 to 199; those for use of a regiment from 200 to 299.

The allotment of reference points within the battalion or regiment is made by the battalion or regimental commander as the case may be.

In allotting "I points" those of the machine gun company are the lowest numbered. The higher numbered "I points" are allotted to the other heavy weapons.

The infantry and artillery should each know the other's reference points and these should be coordinated.

5. Infantry pioneers and their co-operation with engineers.

The infantry pioneer platoons must be provided in good time with any special materials which they may require and be in a position to carry out their work with the simple tools at their disposal.

They can be used for the following work:—

(a) Clearing roads and making temporary bridges over small streams.

(b) Constructing obstacles against enemy tanks and infantry.[*]

(c) Constructing defensive works, light and splinter-proof shelters, O.Ps., obstacles, etc.

(d) Removing enemy obstacles of all sorts.

(e) Clearing passages through obstacles and destroying embrasures when assault detachments attack permanent fortifications.

(f) Making arrangements for gas detection and the decontamination of ground over small areas.

Engineers will be used to carry out more difficult tasks. They will be attached for a limited time to an infantry regiment, e.g., to remove extensive obstacles, particularly mine-fields; to build defensive works; to give support in attacks on permanent fortifications and strong points and to bridge streams. For the more extensive work Labour Corps units may be attached to the engineers.

Engineers employed in a sector, even when they may not be placed under the orders of the infantry, must maintain contact with the responsible infantry commander and inform him of any important work which they are carrying out which may affect the infantry.

---

[*] *Note by the General Staff.*—In the German army mine-fields are laid by engineers.

6. Co-operation with the Air Force.

Wireless communication with the Air Force is not possible unless the divisional signals battalion provides the infantry with the necessary W/T instruments.

Direct communication between the infantry and aircraft is necessary when the aircraft are supporting the land fighting. Aircraft then attack enemy points of resistance, strong points, concentrations—possibly of tanks—and artillery positions with bombs and machine-gun fire with the object of destroying them and at the same time undermining the enemy's will to resist. The infantry must exploit such attacks rapidly and vigorously if it is to achieve its object. If aircraft are employed to support land operations the infantry F.D.Ls. must be clearly indicated by ground signals. This must be done without special orders at the time fixed for the air attack. If no time has been fixed for the air attack, the infantry must indicate its advanced line as soon as friendly aircraft appear.*

Other ground signals for aircraft may be laid down by the higher command or they may possibly be arranged between the infantry and the Air Force direct.

7. Anti-aircraft defence.

All troops must be constantly ready to defend themselves against air attack.

Troops may be ordered to increase their intervals and distances to reduce the effect of air attack, but units must always remain under the immediate control of their commanders.

The battalion has in its M.Gs. and rifles the means of effectively defending itself against low flying aircraft. Infantry weapons are not effective against aircraft flying at high altitudes, but high altitude attacks will usually only be delivered when the battalion is passing through defiles, etc.

M.Gs. and L.M.Gs. are effective against aircraft up to a maximum range of 1,100 yards. If fire from the largest possible number of rifles is concentrated, it may be effective up to 550 yards and frequently obtains material and moral results which are more effective than those of M.G. fire.

When the rifle is used as an anti-aircraft weapon, the rifles of a platoon or at least a section must be concentrated. The fire of a single rifle against aircraft is quite ineffective, leads to mistakes being made, and is therefore prohibited.

---

* *Note by the General Staff.*—The Germans attach great importance to forward troops indicating their positions to the air if they are to be given close support from the air.
Information on a method of ground to air signalling adopted by the German army is contained in "Periodical Notes on the German Army No. 28".

If nothing has been laid down by the regimental or battalion commander, unit commanders decide the number of M.G. and L.M.G. and possibly also the number of rifle platoons which are to be used for anti-aircraft defence.

The number of weapons to be allotted to anti-aircraft defence depends on the likelihood of air attack, the situation, and ground.

In battle, every platoon commander may utilise M.Gs. for defence against air attack whenever the situation and the task in hand permit. Section commanders may also order their sections to engage aircraft with their rifles.

If anti-aircraft defence is to be effective it is essential that all troops should be warned in time of the approach of hostile aircraft, and for this purpose it is essential to have trained personnel as air sentries. Air sentries report to platoon commanders whose responsibility it is to decide whether to give the order "Air-Attack." When this order is given, personnel detailed for anti-aircraft defence take up their positions and are themselves responsible for opening fire at the correct moment. Anti-gas measures are also taken.

If enemy aircraft are carrying out a gas spray attack—which is only possible from aircraft flying very low, at less than 350ft.—the order "Gas Attack" must be given. Troops adjust their respirators and protect themselves with their "gasplane" (anti-gas capes—a square of gas-proof material or paper). Personnel detailed for anti-aircraft defence then engage the enemy aircraft, leaving off their "gas-plane" if necessary.[*]

It is always essential for effective anti-aircraft defence that each man should know exactly what he is to do in the case of an air attack.

8. Co-operation with tanks.

Tanks generally attack in two waves. Usually the task of the first wave is first to destroy A.Tk. guns and then to attack the artillery. The second wave attacks the enemy infantry and destroys them.

In addition detached tank units may be allotted to infantry regiments to break down rapidly any enemy resistance which shows itself after the attack by the second wave of tanks.

---

[*] *Note by the General Staff.*—Although the Germans appear to teach that gas spray is only possible from low altitudes, it is not safe to assume from this that medium or high spray will not be employed by them. It is interesting to note that they teach their troops to adjust their respirators when sprayed. This may be to protect the eyes, in which case it is felt that action will not be quick enough to prevent drops entering the eyes and causing permanent blindness. Our teaching is that on no account must respirators be adjusted, because there is no immediate vapour danger and because it is important to keep the respirator from becoming contaminated. We protect the eyes with eyeshields.

A 10.5cm field howitzer firing on the Kerch front, Crimea, April 1942. The photo was taken by a *Propagandakompanie* photographer and distributed by the German Army. There were several models of 10.5cm howitzer, early types having a range of about 12,000m.

When an attack is to be carried out with limited tank support, the tanks may frequently have to attack in one wave, which must in that case engage both the enemy A.Tk. defence and the enemy infantry.

Die 8,8 cm Flak 18 auf Kreuzlafette.

Beschreibung des Geschützes (Bild 21 und 22).

Die Hauptteile des Geschützes sind:

   die K r e u z l a f e t t e,
   die L a f e t t e,
   das R o h r, V e r s c h l u ß u n d A n s e t z e r.

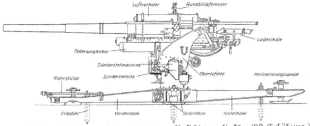

Bild 21. 8,8 cm Flak 18 auf Kreuzlafette — Ansicht von links. (0° Erhöhung.)

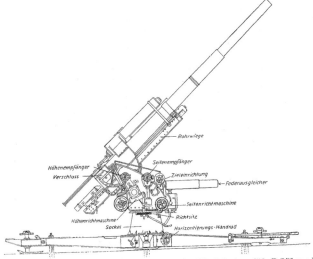

Bild 22. 8,8 cm Flak 18 auf Kreuzlafette. (Ansicht bei etwa 45° Erhöhung.)

The 8.8 cm Flak 18 from the German manual *Handbuch für den Flakartilleristen*, Berlin 1936. With a semi-automatic breech this anti-aircraft gun was capable of up to fifteen rounds a minute. Later it was also used very effectively against tanks, with new models of both gun and ammunition increasing performance during the course of the war.

Every effort must always be made to ensure that a tank attack is a surprise attack, in order to give the enemy as little time as possible to strengthen his A.Tk. defences in the sector attacked.

The moment at which the tank attack is to be launched depends on which of the following methods of attack is chosen:—

(a) Combined attack by infantry and armoured formations to obtain a break-through.

(b) Attack by armoured formations after the infantry has penetrated into the enemy position with the object of converting the penetration into a break-through.

(c) Attack by armoured formations without immediate infantry co-operation.

The essential characteristic of an attack with tanks is mutual support by infantry and tanks. Apart from the greater importance of neutralising A.Tk. weapons, infantry carry out an attack with tank support on the same principles as an attack without tank support. The paralysing effect of tanks breaking into the enemy's defence must be utilised by the infantry as quickly and as boldly as possible for its own advance.

The advance of the second wave of tanks against the enemy gives the infantry fresh support, which may be particularly effective. The infantry should effect its break into the enemy positions *at latest* with this second wave. So long as it possibly can, infantry should keep well up with the second wave, taking full advantage of its support to destroy the enemy, and thus achieve a break through.

In an attack with tank support, infantry must be particularly careful to guard against enemy weapons firing from a flank of the sector to be attacked, for this flanking fire may separate the infantry from the tanks. It is for this reason generally necessary to allot to certain heavy infantry weapons and certain artillery on the flanks of the attacking tanks the task of neutralising any such flanking fire.

If the infantry is separated from the second wave of tanks, it will continue the attack with the support of the tank unit attached to it. This unit will move, as ordered by the regimental commander, either as a complete unit under the orders of its own commander, or by sections attached to battalions either with or immediately after the leading infantry units. At the same time advantage of the ground should be taken so that the advance of the infantry can be observed.

If enemy resistance holds up the infantry advance, the tank company (or sections of it) either on its own initiative, at the request of the infantry or on the order of the regimental or battalion commander goes forward and destroys the enemy by fire at close range. These tanks then wait until the following infantry comes up.

If the infantry loses contact with the tanks, it must continue the attack alone.

Ground which is unsuitable for tanks, or enemy antitank defences—in particular anti-tank obstacles—may make it necessary to hold back the attack by the armoured formations until the infantry has broken into the enemy lines.

Tanks can also be employed without immediate infantry co-operation to exploit certain favourable opportunities. These opportunities may arise particularly when the enemy is fighting a delaying action, in the pursuit and in the retreat. Tanks can then attack without waiting for the infantry, utilising their speed to the full.

Close liaison between the tanks and the infantry is a necessary condition for the effective co-operation of the two arms. The following measures must be taken:—

(a) A pre-arranged plan should be drawn up as soon as possible between the commanders of the two arms.

(b) Attachment of armoured liaison detachments to infantry regiments.

(c) Marking the location of infantry H.Q. (down to platoon H.Q.) by pre-arranged signals.

(d) Indication of objectives by the infantry on the ground.

The armoured liaison detachments consist of an officer with a tank fitted with W/T and a certain number of despatch riders.

9. Anti-tank defence.

The regimental commander will base his orders for the employment of the A.Tk. company on the reconnaissance carried out by its commander.

The 2 cm. (·79 in.) A.A. guns which are placed at the disposal of the infantry are effective against tanks up to 550 yds.; the light infantry guns can be used at ranges over 330 yds. against light armour and tracks, the heavy infantry guns can be used against concentrations of tanks and to defend their own positions. Explosive charges, antitank ditches (at distances of 100–350 yards), rifles and M.Gs. may also be used.

In drawing up a co-ordinated plan for anti-tank defence, the nature of the ground, obstacles and anti-tank weapons must be considered.

In anti-tank defence the decisive factor may be to recognise the imminence of a tank attack as soon as possible and to warn all troops. Special reconnaissance units, in addition to the usual means of reconnaissance, may be employed for this purpose.

C. INFANTRY IN DEFENCE AGAINST TANKS.
(From a German semi-official publication.)

1. The sound of the engines generally gives warning of tank attacks, although this sound may sometimes be drowned by the general noise of battle. On dry ground, the approach of attacking tanks may frequently be recognised from the dust thrown up. The enemy will seek to achieve surprise in delivering his tank attacks. For this purpose he may take advantage of the half-light of early morning or late evening, or of mist or smoke.[*]

2. On the appearance of enemy A.F.Vs., the best means of protection for men armed with L.M.Gs. and rifles is to take cover at once and keep still. In this way the infantryman can keep out of sight of the enemy A.F.V. and out of its effective field of fire, and is also protected from the fire of his own A.Tk. weapons. The new anti-tank rifle issued to rifle companies is effective up to 300 yards.

3. During lectures, the effect of A.P. ammunition against the various lightly armoured A.F.Vs. will be studied. At very close ranges normal S.A.A. fired at the slits and flaps may be effective against the crew of the A.F.V. on account of its splinter effect.

4. Enemy A.F.Vs. which have broken down will be engaged with the A.Tk. rifle. Full advantage must however be taken of the dead ground affording cover from the A.F.V.'s guns. Fire will be directed against the slits and flaps. Hand-grenades may be thrown against and under and in front of the tracks.

5. The infantry-man must not allow his determination to hold his position to be shaken by the appearance of enemy A.F.Vs. Infantry-men caught within the effective range of enemy A.F.Vs. who try to escape by running must expect to be killed. Only when a single A.F.V. is advancing directly on a man will he be able to save himself by jumping aside.

---

[*] *Note by the General Staff.*—The Germans pay particular attention to avoiding loss of surprise by drowning the noise of their own tanks with the sound of artillery fire and low-flying aircraft.

6. Infantry attacking with A.F.Vs. must always be engaged. The object is to separate the enemy infantry from the A.F.Vs. supporting them.

D. ANTI-TANK GUN EMPLACEMENT.
(From a German manual.)

Plates 1 and 2 are reproductions from a German manual showing the method of construction of an anti-tank gun emplacement and the means by which the gun can be concealed when not in action.

When the gun is not required to fire it is concealed underground (Plate 1) and is brought into action in a shallow pit or behind a quickly constructed bank of earth (Plate 2).

Slit trenches of the normal type are dug near but separate from the emplacement. These provide cover for the gun crew and give the maximum protection from bombs, shells and enemy A.F.V. action.

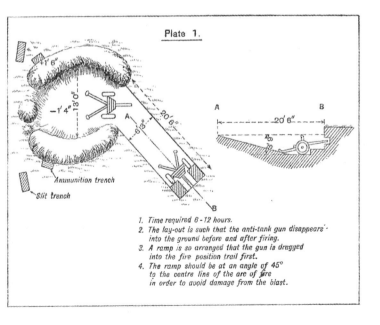

Plate 1.

Ammunition trench

Slit trench

1. Time required 6 - 12 hours.
2. The lay-out is such that the anti-tank gun disappears into the ground before and after firing.
3. A ramp is so arranged that the gun is dragged into the fire position trail first.
4. The ramp should be at an angle of 45° to the centre line of the arc of fire in order to avoid damage from the blast.

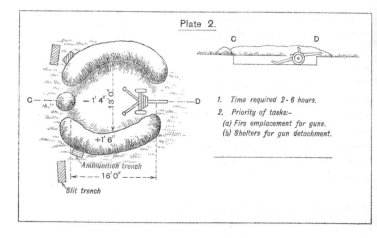

Plate 2.

1. *Time required 2-6 hours.*
2. *Priority of tasks:-*
   (a) Fire emplacement for guns.
   (b) Shelters for gun detachment.

E. CO-OPERATION BETWEEN THE GERMAN AIR FORCE AND ARMY.

1. The role of the German Air Force in co-operation with the army.

(a) *General.*—The main role of the German Air Force, as has been evident from the campaigns in Poland, Norway and France, is to give the maximum support to the German army and enable it to carry out its tasks. The full strength of the Air Force has been devoted to this task in the recent operations in France. The action of the Air Force may take the form of indirect or direct support of the army.

(b) *Indirect support.*—Indirect support is rather a wide term and difficult to define. In general it may be said to include distant reconnaissance of enemy territories and seas, the bombing of enemy bases, sea and land communications, telegraph and telephone systems, dumps, aerodromes and industrial centres, war industries—more especially aircraft industries. If in the opinion of the German High Command demoralization of enemy forces can be attained by the bombing of the civil population, such a step would undoubtedly be taken. In general, only those objectives are bombed, however, the destruction of which would have an indirect influence on the operations of the army. The theory that there is such a thing as separate air strategy is believed to be rejected by the German General Staff.

(c) *Direct support.*—By direct support is meant close reconnaissance and army co-operation work, bombing of enemy concentrations, reserves, headquarters, rear services, road and rail communications, bombing and machine-gunning of enemy ground forces and especially their artillery and antitank positions, the occupation of points of tactical importance by parachute troops and the prevention by fighter aircraft and anti-aircraft defences of enemy reconnaissance and army co-operation. In particular the employment of aircraft in direct support of swift-moving armoured formations should be noted. Moreover, the German Air Force is used to supply mobile formations such as armoured and motorized divisions with petrol, ammunition and supplies.

2. Methods by which the German Air Force carries out its role.

(a) *General.*—In order to facilitate the close co-operation between the Air Force and the army, small Air Force staffs are attached to army formations on the following scale:—

One lieutenant-general and staff per group of armies.

One major-general or colonel and staff per army.

These officers are known as "Koluft" officers.

It is possible that small staffs or liaison officers are also attached to lower formations as circumstances demand.

(b) *Indirect support by the German Air Force.*—The German methods of indirect support are similar to those of our own Air Force.

(c) *Direct support by the German Air Force.*—This is carried out chiefly by medium and dive-bomber aircraft. The Germans have made an extensive study of dive-bomber aircraft, and, from recent experience, it appears that they use it as a form of highly mobile artillery. Dive-bombers can release their bombs with great accuracy and when suitable targets present themselves attacks are carried out continuously by waves of aircraft. Dive-bomber units are allotted to commanders of attacking forces and are used to:—

(i) bomb enemy forward positions as a preliminary to attack,

(ii) bomb enemy centres of resistance and especially their anti-tank positions,

(iii) neutralize enemy artillery,

(iv) in conjunction with fighter aircraft to bomb and machine-gun enemy reinforcements, break up counter-attacks before they develop and destroy retiring enemy ground forces.

They carry out the above tasks quickly and effectively when called upon to do so. As an example, dive-bomber aircraft on one occasion attacked an enemy centre of resistance less than 30 minutes after the forward elements of the German ground troops had called for assistance. In short, dive-bomber aircraft carry out to a great extent tasks which had previously been assigned to heavy and long range artillery.

During the attack, and particularly while the artillery is moving from position to position, dive-bombers and fighter aircraft engage the enemy throughout the depth of the position. The principal task of the Air Force in such an attack is to prevent the enemy reserves from being moved up to stop the break-through. The air intelligence liaison units provide the necessary signal equipment and accompany the first waves of attacking infantry and keep the Air Force constantly informed of the exact position of their own front line.

F. METHOD OF ATTACK ON A PORT.

A competent observer who was in Norway at the time of the German invasion and personally witnessed two German landings has given a description of the methods adopted.

These methods were peculiarly successful against Norway where no attack was expected and where the defence was not properly organized.

At each landing witnessed the methods adopted and the sequence of events were precisely the same. Open beaches were never used, except as a diversion, the landings being made at a quay in each case. The time chosen was between 0200 and 0230 hours, this being the darkest part of the night.

The first intimation was a series of magnesium flares dropped from aircraft over the permanent defences. This was followed within 20 or 30 seconds by heavy and accurate bombing of the gun defences. Simultaneously with this bombing, the first sea-borne flight arrived. This invariably consisted of light vessels of about the size of large fishing craft. No attempt was made to neutralize the gun defences by landing, and complete reliance seemed to be placed on neutralizing them by aircraft during the passage of the first and subsequent flights of ships.

The next event was the lighting of the quays of the port by magnesium flares, followed immediately by very heavy and accurate attacks by many dive-bombing planes on the extremities of the quays, where machine-gun posts would normally be expected to be found. Immediately subsequent to this, the first ships arrived at the quay and made fast.

The first ship contained soldiers armed with grenades. These men jumped ashore flinging their grenades in all directions and clearing a passage for the men disembarking from the following vessels.

Subsequent vessels landed machine-guns, light A.A. guns and light tanks; these last were carried athwart ships and chocked up so as to be at the correct quay level for the state of the tide.

The object was to put the quay defences out of action before material was landed, and reliance seems to have been placed almost entirely on the very heavy bombing and prolific and indiscriminate use of hand grenades by the first men ashore.

Having got men and material ashore, the Germans seemed content to advance into the town and sit tight waiting for further reinforcements in heavier ships. They relied on the presence of the civilian population all around them to prevent air retaliation.

Simultaneous with the above action, it was the usual practice to organize diversions in the shape of beach landings on the immediate flanks and parachutists' descents behind the ports.

From the time the quays were first lit up by the flares it was reckoned that within 30 minutes the Germans would expect to land about 1,600 men.

G. THE EFFECT OF REFUGEES ON MILITARY OPERATIONS.

Detailed reports have now been received regarding the evacuation of a large proportion of the population of Paris and the consequent effect upon the roads.

The exodus *en masse* began upon the sight of a vast pall of smoke upon the horizon heralding the approach of the Germans. Rumours also set in motion streams of refugees in quite remote back areas with the result that when military traffic finally should have got clear of the refugees it encountered all the refugee difficulties all over again. The refugees had such an effect on the roads that one military car took 14½ hours to cover 25 miles.

Refugee traffic paid no attention to "black-out" orders at night, and the lights shown attracted enemy bombing. This in turn increased the confusion, for even if no hits were registered the refugees, upon the commencement of bombing, left their driverless cars to block the road and hid in the ditches.

A direct hit on a road on one occasion caused a delay of 2½ hours while wounded and debris were moved. It was not possible to provide ambulances for refugee casualties as, coming from the rear, they were moving against the stream of traffic.

When 200 miles had been covered from Paris another form of traffic jam set in, caused by refugees running out of petrol. These people simply abandoned their cars and continued their flight on foot.

In general, refugee traffic could only be kept in motion and in some form of control by a certain degree of ruthlessness and disregard of sentimental considerations. Any vehicle which broke down had to be got off the road at once. Any relaxation led to jams and attracted enemy aircraft.

It was fatal to delay any pre-arranged scheme of demolitions out of consideration for the refugees.

H. PHYSICAL TRAINING FOR FRONT-LINE TROOPS.
(From a German semi-official publication.)

1. General principles.
Physical training for front-line troops should as far as possible be recreational. Physical exercises which are unwillingly carried out fail in their object. Over-strain must be avoided.

The P.T. officer must, however, choose games and exercises which are both recreational and health promoting.

If a unit is withdrawn from the line for some time, P.T. should at first be mainly recreational but gradually graded up to serious work. Even in this process the recreational aspect may be preserved by means of competitions and displays.

2. Organisation.
The aim must be to keep all the men continuously employed. This is best done by keeping the groups down to 20–25 men.

Games and exercises must as far as possible take the form of competitions, and in particular competitions between teams representing existing units, e.g. gun detachments, gunners v. drivers etc.

Two hours (including going to and from the sports ground, dressing and undressing) is the shortest period which can be usefully devoted to P.T.

Attention should be paid to hygiene (cooling off after strenuous effort, washing, pedicure, etc.).

The disinclination, particularly of older soldiers, for everything connected with P.T. will soon be overcome if senior officers take part in it and thus set an example.

3. Ground and equipment.

Dry meadow land without shell holes is best, but almost any ground will serve.

Simple gymnastic equipment can often be improvised without difficulty. Footballs, hand balls, and punch balls are easily obtainable and can be carried with the unit.

4. Dress.

The usual dress for sport is a cotton vest, shorts and gym shoes. In warm weather P.T. can be carried out in swimming suits and bare-footed.

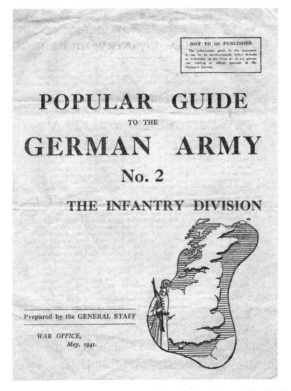

The *Popular Guide* series ran alongside *Periodical Notes*, giving brief summaries of specific subjects. Issue 2 of May 1941 attempted to encapsulate the German infantry division in just six pages and two diagrams.

5. Forms of physical training.

P.T. can take the following forms:—

(a) *Free movements.*—Free movements can be easily carried out almost anywhere. Simple exercises should be chosen which can be grasped without difficulty. Suitably filled sand-bags can be used instead of medicine-balls.

(b) *Games.*—Many games can be played even in gun positions and wagon-lines, and are particularly suitable for older men. Examples—tug of war, wrestling and throwing, sack races (feet bound together if sacks are not available), chariot races, tilting, etc.

Several army blankets laid on top of each other will provide an excellent mat for wrestling etc. Putting the weight (with various improvised weights) is possible even in gun positions and wagon-lines. High and long jumping can be carried out wherever it is possible to dig a pit.

(c) *Running:*

    (i)   Sprint-races up to 100–200 yards.

    (ii) Obstacle races, either over natural obstacles or obstacles improvised from vehicles etc.

    (iii) Cross-country runs. These are often unpopular with the men, but they are particularly valuable for developing endurance. Only the younger men should be sent on cross-country runs, and the distances at first should be short with frequent intervals during which the men are allowed to walk.

    (iv) Runs through woods are the best form of cross-country running, and older men can also take part. The men are allowed to walk and run alternately, and walk up all hills.

    (v) Hare and hounds.

    (vi) Relay races.

(d) *Gymnastic exercises.*—Wherever equipment is available or can be improvised.

(e) *Weight-lifting.*—With improvised weights.

(f) *Bathing and swimming.*—In warm weather no opportunity should be missed for bathing and swimming. Wherever possible a stream should be dammed and kept free of slime by means of gratings. Every opportunity should also be taken for sun-bathing.

(g) *Competitions.*—Competitions make P.T. much more interesting. Competitions between teams are preferable to competitions between individuals. Finals should, if possible, be made festive occasions.

(h) *Excursions.*—Excursions on foot to places of interest in the neighbourhood appeal to the older men and reservists.

I. GERMAN MORALE.

1. The morale of the German army.

(a) *At the outbreak of the war.*—The youth of the army was composed of men thoroughly Nazi-minded, having experienced the most impressionable years of its life under the regime of the Third Reich. Its early training in the Hitler Youth organization and subsequent compulsory labour service, and the moral pressure and obligations associated with them, inspired loyalty to the army and the regime. With few exceptions, this spirit was shared by the older reservists called to the colours. The success of the campaign in Poland strengthened further the faith alike of recruit and reservist in the Führer, the Party leaders and, above all, in the army in which he served. Morale, consequently, was at a very high level.

(b) *During the period of static warfare.*—The comparative inactivity which followed the Polish campaign had no very pronounced effect upon the morale of the army, though there were indications that it was not quite on the same high level as before. This lowering of morale and discipline was not due, as a rule, to discontent with conditions in the Service. There existed during this period considerable ill-feeling between the army and the S.S. and a certain amount of dissension between the army and Party leaders. These factors may have contributed less towards the slight weakening of morale than did the "ennui" occasioned by comparative inactivity and the economic conditions in the home country.

Restrictions and hardships resulting from the suddenly imposed rationing of food, fuel, clothes, shortage of many of the necessities of life (and their substitution by "Ersatz" articles), enemy propaganda, and the growing realization that the war was to last longer than had been anticipated, all contributed towards a lowering of the spirit of the civilian population and were probably not entirely without influence upon the morale of the soldier.

Reliable information, however, points to the fact that during the month of February, there were only 38 cases of desertion from the army and 102 cases of absence without leave, or over-staying leave—figures which speak for themselves in an army of, at that time, approximately five and a half millions of men. An examination of reports of prisoners of war who were taken during that period showed that the morale of the front line troops was, on the whole, good, but that the same spirit and discipline was less noticeable among troops in the home formations and particularly among the older men.*

(c) *The morale of the army to-day.*—In the same way as the success of the Polish campaign stimulated military morale the successful operations in Norway, Denmark, Holland and Belgium, culminating with France's capitulation, have been responsible for raising the standard of morale to a high level.

Operations in which S.S. divisions have fought side by side with ordinary infantry divisions have had the effect of improving relations between the two services. Implicit faith in the Führer and belief that he can do no wrong would appear to have removed any real dissension between the army and Party. The army, though possibly unaware of it, at all events in the lower ranks, seems now to be permeated with Party.

If economic conditions in the home country have not improved, they no longer seem to influence the morale of the soldier to the same extent as they did during the period of static warfare.

Generally speaking, there exists a spirit of "Kamaraderie" between officers and other ranks. Indeed, strict discipline does not exclude, as it did under the old regime, human contact between officer and man. The food of the soldier is sufficient and compares favourably with that of a highly paid worker in the heavy industry. No serious or organized complaints in respect of pay or leave have been noted.

The morale of a unit varies according to the locality from which its personnel is drawn and it is not surprising to learn that that of the Austrian troops is lower than that of the Prussian or Bavarian. Weakening of discipline among men of Bavarian units has, however, also been reported, but in these reports and others which speak of poor morale, reference is made to isolated cases only.

The numerous reports available make it difficult to sift truth from rumour, but there is good evidence that former Austrian officers criticised their employment in the most dangerous operations and that Austrian troops in Norway have protested their unwillingness to be used in an invasion of Great Britain and that severe disciplinary action had to be taken against them.

Note by the General Staff.—Since this note was written there are indications that a number of factors have contributed during recent weeks towards a certain weakening of morale in elements of the German army, particularly among units stationed in Norway and the coastal sectors of France and Belgium.

Another reliable source reported the weakening of discipline and morale, resulting from a French attack, among soldiers of German units holding the Siegfried line in the Saar in June. It is believed that the units in question were newly-formed reserve and Landwehr.

Though credence may be given to some of the reports of the increase of crime and serious offences among soldiers and the severe measures which are being taken to suppress it, it must be borne in mind that, in all cases, these occurrences have been in one or the other of Germany's newly occupied territories. The parading of numbers of handcuffed soldiers through the streets of towns (of which several reports have been received) may have had for its purpose the impression upon the civilian population of Germany's sense of justice. The crime in most cases is said to have been that of looting.

Other instances of the weakening of morale and discipline have been brought to notice. Generally speaking, however, recent reports on the interrogation of prisoners point to a high standard of morale. This applies also to the Air Force and parachutists.

Most prisoners would welcome a speedy conclusion of the war. They have complete faith in the Führer and unshaken belief in Germany's ability to bring this about by successful invasion of this country.

2. Civilian morale in Germany.

Despite the fact that the "Home Front" is, in these days, so regimented that the difference between the morale of the civilians and the morale of the armed forces is less apparent than would otherwise be the case, the contrast undoubtedly exists, and redounds to the credit of the soldier.

This may be due, in part, to the fact that the soldier rarely comes into contact with those elements, small though they be, which are not partisans of the regime and which consist mainly of the professional classes, the Church and intellectuals. Also, the soldier is not in close touch with conditions at home.

If recent military successes have acted as a stimulant upon the army, they would appear to have created, at home, surprisingly little popular enthusiasm for the continuation of the war. It is felt that these victories have not resulted in any appreciable improvement of economic conditions and there is an increasing feeling that Germany has subjugated larger populations than she can conveniently cope with. People are discouraged by the prospect of a poor harvest and the possibility of having to face another winter with short rations of food and coal. Continual air raids upon the industrial areas are affecting output and having an exhausting effect on the population. Many families are without news of husbands and sons, and it is generally believed that casualties in the army, navy and Air Force have been much heavier than indicated by official reports.

Despite all this there exists among the masses undiminished faith in their leaders and a determination to submit to further hardships as their contribution towards the price of victory.

3. Conclusion.

(a) *Military morale.*—On the whole, the morale of the army continues to be of a high order and discipline has not relaxed to any marked extent. Differences between the High Command and Party leaders, if they exist, are no longer subjects for discussion, while the ill-feeling which existed between the army and the S.S. appears to have been set aside. Above all, the army has complete faith in Hitler and belief that victory will be theirs.

(b) *Civilian morale.*—In spite of Germany's successes, economic conditions in the home country, the growing fear that another winter of war may have to be faced, casualties and the effects of air raids on Germany are undoubtedly causing uneasiness among the population. The spirit of the people, though somewhat shaken, is one of determination to work for victory. Morale is unlikely to be undermined so long as the public retains its present faith in Hitler.

Current morale issues include:—

(*a*) The desire of older men to get home without having to face another winter with the army.

(*b*) The dangers which lie before soldiers in the proposed attempt at invasion of this country. Fear of the water and a premonition of impending failure following all their recent successes.

(*c*) Disquieting letters from home, including references to effect of our air bombing.

(*d*) In northern Norway, the climate, which is said to be too rigorous in winter.

(*e*) In Norway and France, the training exercises, including embarking and disembarking with small craft and fishing boats intended for the invasion of this country, swimming exercises and the general idea of being employed in an undertaking which does not appeal and in which casualties are bound to be very high.

Of these, item (*e*) would appear to be responsible more than any other for such lowering of morale as has been brought to notice.

Signs of this weakening of discipline and morale, and descriptions of the disciplinary measures taken to counter it have formed the subject of many reports. These, however, with few exceptions, are not eye-witness observations but accounts based upon information obtained at second hand. They include such incidents as mass desertion and open rebellion resulting in the execution of many soldiers in Norway; the mutiny of troops in a coastal sector of France and their transport, handcuffed together, to Germany; the finding of the bodies of a large number of suicides washed up on the coasts and floating on the rivers of Norway and France.

While there would appear to be an element of truth underlying these reports, made in good faith, it is thought that all are stories which lend themselves to exaggeration, and a careful examination of all reports forces us to the assumption that full advantage has, in most cases, been taken of this licence.

Concurrently with these adverse reports, others, pointing to the sustained high morale and standard of discipline in the German army, continue to be received from sources believed to be reliable. To these may be added the impressions obtained from the interrogation of recently captured German Air Force prisoners. These reports indicate that, while there appears to be some dissatisfaction with such matters as rewards, promotion and the lack of training of personnel and, to a lesser degree, with the higher strategy of those in authority, which is resulting in unnecessary losses, morale generally, if not of the same high standard as was shown three months ago, is still of a very high order.

CONCLUSIONS.

There are indications that a number of factors have led to a certain weakening of morale in elements of the German army, particularly among units stationed in Norway and the coastal sectors of France and Belgium. It is not thought that the morale of the German army, as a whole, is likely to be affected to any extent by isolated instances of dissatisfaction among certain of its units. Dissatisfied elements will be dealt with by Nazi methods which will ensure no spreading of discontent, and they will be replaced by others whose fighting qualities and morale, like that of the German army generally, are still believed to be of a very high order.

J. GERMAN TOPOGRAPHICAL CONVENTIONAL SIGNS.
(FROM A GERMAN DOCUMENT.)

The chart, reproduced from a captured document, shows conventional signs which it is believed are used in large-scale German maps.

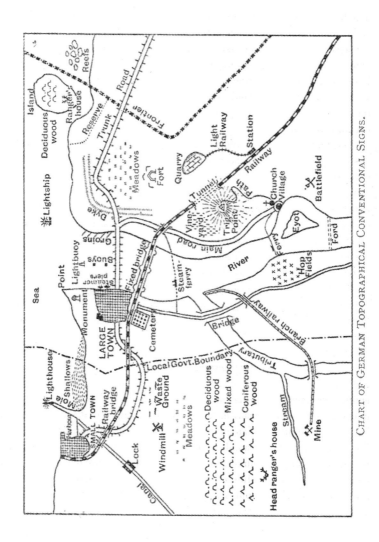

CHART OF GERMAN TOPOGRAPHICAL CONVENTIONAL SIGNS.

CHAPTER 2

Preliminary Report on the Panzer I, Model B 1943

The best way to learn about enemy tanks was to capture them, complete and in running order, with talkative crewmen – and a manual. Next to this, damaged vehicles could be taken apart by experts. The result was not just knowledge of the German Army, but crucial inspiration for Allied designers. Early in the war as a victorious enemy advanced across Europe, few tanks were available for first-hand examination, and much had to be learned through third parties and the press, as well as by espionage and reports from occupied countries.

The war in North Africa with its dramatic advances and retreats changed all this very quickly. With the Italians on the verge of defeat, Mussolini called upon his German allies for support, and so the *Afrika Korps* under Rommel arrived early in 1941. Armour was deployed in strength, and soon German vehicles were being captured, some being examined or reused in the field, others shipped back to the UK for more thorough examination. As the war progressed, other campaigns produced new samples as Allied forces advanced. The technical branch of British military intelligence, MI10, was active in gathering information on the hardware; MI14 collected data on the German order of battle.

A key player in establishing and disseminating information was the School of Tank Technology, a new branch of the Military College of Science founded in 1942. By June that year the school was sharing the site of the old RAF Chobham camp in Surrey with the 'Fighting Vehicle Proving Establishment', and about 37 acres of the surrounding common were requisitioned for vehicle testing. From this period onward the School of Tank Technology produced a series of booklets, somewhat misleadingly entitled 'Preliminary Reports', on specific vehicles. What was odd about the title was the fact that in many instances the booklet was not the first report, but a rewrite or update of an initial report in the light of fresh examination. For example, as the preamble to publication 13, on the Lorraine self-propelled 15 cm gun mounting, observed, it did 'little more than elaborate on the report made by Middle East on this vehicle, and confirms certain statements, which without stripping various components, were then necessarily of a speculative nature'.

The *Landwirtschaftlicher Schlepper* of 1934 was a light armoured turretless
'tractor' intended as a training vehicle which did not break the letter,
but certainly infringed the spirit, of the Treaty of Versailles. The same
hull and suspension were used for the first model of the Panzer I.

The Panzer I during manoeuvres, from the German 'collector work'
Adolf Hitler 1931–1935: Pictures from the Life of the Führer, published in
Germany in 1936. German censors have obscured unit markings, but this
was just one of many images freely available to intelligence analysts.

Nevertheless the reports of the school were a growing source of knowledge. Particularly significant were numbers 7 and 15, both on the Panzer IV. No. 7, of 1942, featured the IV D, captured in North Africa, and no. 15, of 1943, covered the Panzer IV 'Special' with its long-barrelled 75 mm gun. No. 16, also produced in 1943, was devoted to the *Sturmgeschütz* ('assault gun') based on the Panzer III chassis. Best known of all was report no. 19, covering the Tiger tank, for while the truth about this beast was worrying enough, analysis helped clear away any amount of speculation. In 1944, report no. 19 itself grew into a whole series of papers covering virtually every aspect of the tank.

MI10 had first become aware a new heavy tank was in production in late 1942 through 'a captured document', soon alerting both the Middle East and the mission in Moscow to look out for details. Some quickly appeared through a 'delicately placed, reliable source', but it was the enemy who provided the first photograph to be seen in Britain in the *National Zeitung* of 11 December 1942. Two Tigers were knocked out in North Africa and examined early in February 1943, and a partial evaluation was soon supplemented by information from prisoners. Brief technical reports followed, and now MI14 was able to add organisational detail. Yet the biggest prize, a Tiger in working order, was not captured until 21 April at Djebel Djaffa, and it was this vehicle that was eventually transported back to the UK for a complete strip down at the School of Tank Technology.

Interestingly the facility also examined the hardware of Allies, obtaining, among other vehicles, a Soviet T-34 in November 1943, and later a French Char B1. As another product of its work, the school produced glossaries of both German and Italian tank terms, intended 'to be useful to those who are engaged in translating technical documents, examining captured material, and interrogating prisoners'. The second edition of the German language glossary, produced in March 1943, contained more than a thousand words or expressions garnered from nineteen captured official publications, four trade instructions and numerous technical journals, as well as by the examination of markings and inscriptions found in captured tanks. Additional sections dealt with abbreviations, imperial and metric conversion, and materials.

As can readily be appreciated, there was no guarantee enemy equipment would be captured in chronological sequence, nor that its condition could allow equally detailed treatment in all cases. So it was with the Panzer I. This vehicle had been the first German tank to go into mass production in the inter-war period, with manufacture commencing as early as 1934. British intelligence was well aware of it by the time of the Spanish Civil War, and its life in a front-line combat role effectively ended in 1941, although some were converted and retained as command vehicles, ammunition carriers and self-propelled guns. Very few of an 'Ausf. F' variant with heavier armour were produced, but further orders were cancelled. Preliminary reports had already appeared on the 'Ausf. A' type, a self-propelled mounting and the command vehicle.

It was therefore remarkable that the School of Tank Technology should have issued a fresh report on a badly damaged Panzer I (B) as late as April 1943. Yet Major Barnes of the Royal Tank Regiment and his collaborator DM Pearse were filling something of a gap in British knowledge. A total of 675 Panzer I (B) types had been produced in 1935 to 1937, and of these 74 were still in service at the time of the invasion of Russia. The new report helped highlight differences between the 'A' and 'B' models, including the longer chassis and changes to the engine and suspension – though the armour was not significantly different.

If it was not already clear by 1943, the various preliminary reports on the pre-war Panzers made it obvious that German success during the *Blitzkrieg* had not been primarily due to some 'miracle weapon'. The Panzer I, in particular, was armed, like British light tanks of the late 1930s, only with machine guns. It moved no faster and its armour was of similar thickness. The Panzers III and IV were much more advanced, but French tanks were more numerous and frequently better armoured. Some of the most important answers therefore lay not in the tanks themselves, but in tactics and collaboration between different arms.

As General Heinz Guderian's book *Achtung – Panzer!* pointed out in 1937, tanks should not be used in driblets, but together with infantry in a great 'combined operation' or within a framework co-operating with other arms. Moreover, armoured forces were to be launched in a 'concentrated surprise attack', accompanied where required by engineers for mine and obstacle clearance. Enemy anti-tank guns would be knocked out by artillery, blinded with smoke, suppressed by machine guns or overwhelmed by mass. The timely intervention of enemy armour was to be prevented not just by surprise and speed but use of the German airforce and long-range artillery to hit communications, roads and assembly areas. Gallingly, at least some of these conclusions had been reached by the study of British methods of 1917 and 1918.

Preliminary   Report   No. 10

GERMAN

Pz.Kw.I
(Model   B)

School of Tank Technology
Egham

April   1943

FOREWORD

The fighting arrangements, turret and front superstructure of this tank are similar to those of the Pz.Kw.I (Model "A"). The chassis and engine are those of the standard Model "B" as found on the S.P. Mounting and Commander's Tank.

FRONT VIEW

THREE-QUARTER NEAR/SIDE VIEW

REAR VIEW

As these features have already been described in S.T.T. Preliminary Reports Nos. 2, 4 and 9, it was not considered necessary to repeat the descriptions in this report and references to particular components will be found on Page 4.

<u>**FRONT VIEW**</u>
<u>**THREE-QUARTER NEAR/SIDE VIEW**</u>
<u>**REAR VIEW**</u>

PRELIMINARY REPORT ON

GERMAN PZ.KW. I. MODEL 'B'

Received from Middle East

EXAMINED AT FARNBOROUGH (D.T.D. No. 3001) March, 1943.

EXAMINERS: MAJOR J.D. BARNES, R.T.R., and MR. D.M. PEARCE, B.A. (Cantab.). D.T.D. PROJECT NO. V.7020

<u>**1. TYPE**</u>
Pz.Kw.I (Model "B").

<u>**2. GENERAL CONDITION**</u>
The vehicle is a non-runner. Both tracks are deficient. The engine compartment has suffered considerable damage by fire, the petrol tanks have exploded and the carburettor and magneto are both rendered unserviceable. The fire has also caused considerable damage to instruments and fittings in the fighting compartment. The armour has not been penetrated.

<u>**3. WEIGHT**</u>
4.8 tons (as received and less tracks, armament, all stowage and various internal fittings). It is estimated that the weight in battle order would be 5.63 tons.

<u>**4. SPEED**</u>
Not tested. Speedometer marking shows maximum speed in top gear as 38 Km.p.h. (23.6 m.p.h.)

5. CREW
Two – Commander/Gunner – Driver.

6. DIMENSIONS
Length, width and height are overall dimensions. Allowance is made for tracks in the height and clearance dimensions.

Length	14′ 0″
Width	6′ 9¼
Height	5′ 8¾
Clearance	10″
Ground Contact	7′ 11″
Track Centres	5′ 6″

7. AMMUNITION CARRIED
The few ammunition bins and magazines that remain in the tank are badly damaged, and it is not possible to determine the amount of S.A.A. carried. As a guide, however, reference may be made to S.T.T. Preliminary Report No. 2 on the Pz.Kw.I (Model "A").

8. OBSERVATION
Observation in the hull superstructure and turret are as on the Pz.Kw. I (Model "A") with the exception that in the offside superstructure there is only one vision port, and in the rear superstructure there are no vision ports.

9. GENERAL CONSTRUCTION
<u>Turret</u> – The construction of the turret is as on the Pz.Kw.I (Model "A").

Internal Dimensions of Turret
Width at top	2′	10″
Width at base	3′	4″
Front to rear at top	3′	1⅞″
Front to rear at base	3′	8¾″
Inside diameter of ring	3′	0½″
Height from floor to turret roof	4′	0″

<u>Superstructure</u> – The construction of the superstructure
is as on the Pz.Kw.I (Model "A").

On each superstructure side plate immediately above the track guard is
bolted an extra 13mm. plate measuring $5'' \times 24''$. It would appear that this
is to give extra protection to S.A.A. stowed at these points in the fighting
compartment. This feature is evidently not peculiar to the Pz.Kw.I (Model "B")
as a photograph from an enemy source shows a model "A" fitted with similar
extra plates.

<u>Hull</u> – The construction of the hull is as on the Pz.Kw.I (Model "B")
Commander's Tank.

10. ARMOUR	BASIC	EXTRA ANGLE
A. Cupola top		
B. Cupola front and sides	No cupola fitted	
C. Turret top front	7 mm.	82°
D. " " rear	7 mm.	90° (Horizontal)
E. " sides	13 mm.	22°
F. " rear	13 mm.	22°
G. " front	15 mm.	8°
H. Gun mantlet	15 mm.	Roller
J. Front vertical plate	12 mm.	22°
K. " glacis plate	8 mm.	(73° upper 70° lower)
L. " nose plate	13 mm.	26°
M. " lower nose plate	Not fitted	
N. Side superstructure	15 mm.	13mm. (see Para.9) 22°
P. " hull plate	15 mm.	0° (Vertical)
Q. Top front plate	8 mm.	90° (Horizontal)
R. " rear plate	6 mm.	87°
S. Top rear engine cover plate		
Rear engine cover		
plate (lower)	—	—
T. Observation cover plate	15 mm.	19°
U. Belly plate (front)	6 mm.	90° (Horizontal)
W. Tail plate (upper)	15 mm.	19°
" " (lower)	15 mm.	56°
X. Skirting plates	Not fitted.	

(The "Angle of Plate" given is the angle between the plate surface and the vertical, which is equal to the "Angle of Impact" for horizontal attack).

11. INSTRUMENTS AND CONTROLS

Drivers controls as in Pz.Kw.I (Model "A")

<u>Instrument Panel</u> – on left

Rev Counter marked V.D.O. Graduated 300 - 3500 (2800–3500 in RED)
(1200–2000 in GREEN)
Centre top - switch (purpose not known)
Key switch under above.
Oil gauge 0– 6 Kg./cm.^{2} - two switches - lighting
Rotary switch reading O.H., V.I., V.2., V.3.,
Speedometer 0 - 50 Km. Total Reading: 00843 Km.
Speeds in gears shown as:
1st = 4½ Km 2nd = 9km. 3rd = 14.75Km 4th = 23.5Km 5th = 38 Km.
Ignition switch and starter button incorporating pilot light.

12. COMMUNICATION

The aerial for the W/T is mounted on the offside front of the superstruoture and may be raised or lowered by a lever, operating through a rod and insulated coupling, to the right of the operator.

The cradle for the wireless set (deficient) is mounted under the glacis plate to the right of the gearbox. A rotary converter and suppressor unit is mounted on the floor of the fighting compartment, slightly behind the cradle for the set.

13. OUTSIDE STOWAGE

Provision for the usual accessories is made on the track guards.

14. RECOGNITION POINTS

The tank is very similar to the Pz.Kw.I (Model "A") except that the engine superstructure is higher and extends back further by about one foot, and a separate idler wheel and four instead of three top rollers are fitted.

15. VULNERABLE POINTS

The turret ring joint is particularly vulnerable there being no deflectors fitted for protection.

The roller gun mantlet might possibly be jammed by M.G. or A/Tk. rifle fire.

<u>Air Intakes and Outlets</u> – are identical with those on the Pz.Kw.I S.P. Mounting.

16. IDENTIFICATION MARKINGS

Colour – Putty
German cross on offside of turret, nearside of superstructure and tailplate.
On Traverse gearbox – S. 792
On junction box over wireless set – Fur Ant-Stecker Auber Batterie L./21
On engine bearer – Motor Nr. 19093. 3791 c.cm.
On Gearbox – ZF.FG.31. Mod. I. 5606 J
Mod. 5605 D

17. REFERENCES

Details are not given where they are similar to those described in S.T.T. Preliminary Reports, Nos. 2, 4 and 9 on the Pz.Kw.I (Model A) S.P. Mounting (Model B) and Commander's Tank (Model B) respectively. References to the particular components are given below.

For details of:

ARMAMENT	
ACCESS DOORS	
TRACKS	See Preliminary Report No. 2
STEERING & FINAL DRIVE	
SPECIAL EQUIPMENT	
TRACK ADJUSTMENT	
ENGINE & AUXILIARIES	See Preliminary Report No.4
GEARBOX & TRANSMISSION	
SUSPENSION	See Preliminary Report Nos. 4 & 9
TOWING ATTACHMENTS	See Preliminary Report No.9

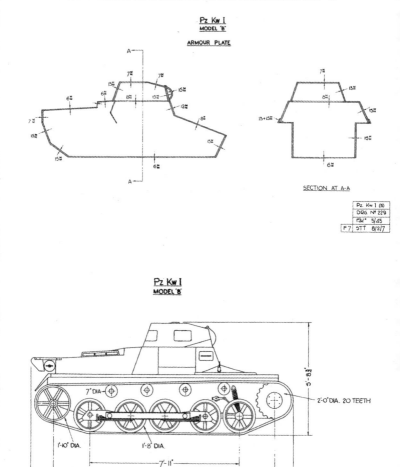

Pz Kw I
MODEL 'B'

ARMOUR PLATE

SECTION AT A-A

	Pz. Kw 1 (B)	
	DRG Nº 229	
	PJW 3/43	
F7	STT 8/2/7	

Pz Kw I
MODEL 'B'

SIDE VIEW

	Pz. Kw. I (B)	
	DRG Nº 228	
	PJW 3/43	
F7	STT 8/2/7	

Pz Kw I
MODEL 'B'

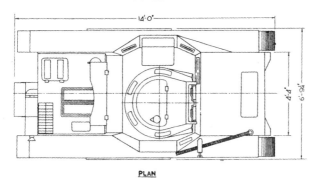

PLAN

	Pz. Kw I (B)	
	DRG. Nº 227	
	FIW	3/43
F7	STT	8/2/7

Pz. Kw. I
MODEL : 'B'

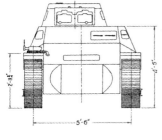

FRONT VIEW

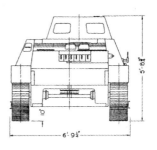

REAR VIEW

	Pz. Kw I (B)	
	DRG. Nº 226.	
	FIW	3/43.
F7	STT	8/2/7

GERMAN TANKS

Light tank   Pz. Kw. II
                                                   Model F

As forecast under " Remarks " at the foot of page 22, the
new model has the superstructure front extending the full
width of the hull.

The rear idler is disc type.

Thickest armour is now 35 mm single skin.

Otherwise very similar in appearance to Pz. Kw. II on
pages 16, 22 and 23

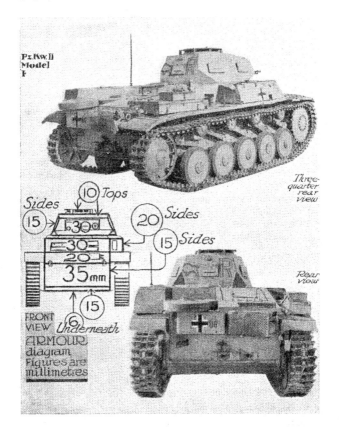

Pz.Kw.II
Model
F

Three-quarter rear view

Sides
(15)
(10) *Tops*
(20) *Sides*
(15) *Sides*

30
30
20
35 mm
(15)
(6) *Underneath*

FRONT VIEW

ARMOUR diagram
Figures are millimetres

Rear view

GERMAN TANKS

German
Light tank
Pz. Kw. II
Model F

Armour, thickest plate		35 mm
Weight laden	..	10 tons
Crew	...	3
Armament, turret	One 2 cm HMG and one MG	
Overall length	...	15 ft 0 in
Overall width	...	7 ft 4 in
Overall height	...	6 ft 6 in
Engine ...	140 bhp petrol	
Speed, road ...	...	30 mph
Radius of action, road		125 miles (estimated)
Trench crossing	...	6 ft 0 in
Step	...	1 ft 6 in
Fording ...	...	3 ft 0 in

The Panzer II, Ausf. F, from *AFV Recognition, Part II, Enemy Turreted AFVs, Amendment 1*, of July 1943. Finding out about German armour, its capabilities and specification was but part of the story. This knowledge had to be digested by intelligence organisations and passed to troops in the field.

The Panzer III, Flammpanzer, or 'flame thrower' tank was a conversion of the Ausf. M type vehicle carried out in early 1943. The projector replaced the main armament and the crew was reduced to three to accommodate fuel tanks, but two machine guns were retained. Originally intended for the Eastern Front, this weapon came as an unpleasant surprise to US troops in Italy; the experience of one US platoon was reported in the *Military Intelligence Bulletin* of July 1944. Under fire from the machine guns of ordinary tanks, the Americans attempted to withdraw, but 'the flame-throwing tanks then joined the action, using their primary weapon against personnel … German infantrymen, equipped with machine pistols, moved forward with the armoured vehicles'.

FLAME THROWER ON Pz. Kw. 3

STANDARD Pz. Kw. 3

Application of knowledge gained by hard experience: the differences
between the flame-throwing tank and the ordinary gun-armed Panzer III.
From the US *Military Intelligence Bulletin*, Vol. 2, no. 11, July 1944.

US troops with a ditched Panzer IV (Ausf. H) near Saint-Lô, Normandy, 1944. The 25-ton Panzer IV remained a mainstay of German tank forces: the 'Ausf. H' variant had 80 mm of frontal armour, and protection was supplemented by side and turret skirts. Its main armament was the 75 mm *Kampfwagenkanone* (*KwK*) 40 L/48 with a semi-automatic breech, capable of penetrating more than 150 mm of armour at close range, given a perpendicular strike.

The 60-ton Tiger I during trials in front of assembled dignitaries, moving with its turret traversed to the rear to prevent the 8.8 cm gun snagging on obstacles. Whether to attempt to keep technology secret or make propaganda of impressive weapons was a continuing dilemma.

German Heavy Cruiser Tank

P O I N T S   F O R

B r o a d s i d e

Turret

Nearly flat topped, sloping down to a rounded gun mantlet, set on a vertical face. Sloping back. Cupola at left rear.

Armament

Very long 7·5 cm gun, fitted with muzzle brake, projecting about 6½ ft in front of tank. No external housing for recoil gear.

Track assembly and suspension

Similar in appearance to Tiger when latter is fitted with narrow tracks, except that the second row of bogie wheels is convex.

Hull

Long flat topped, with superstructure front and glacis plate combined in one clean slope. Overhanging rear superstructure.

Remarks : Note similarity of hull design to the Russian T.34. Submersible like the Tiger. Streamlined and fairly fast. Owing to the presence of rear access door in the turret, the fitting of a stowage bin in this position is unlikely.

Amdt 1
Nov 1 43

Pz.Kw.V " Panther "

R E C O G N I T I O N

H e a d - o n

Flat topped, sloping sided and centrally placed with rectangular front.
Smoke dischargers on each side.

7·5 cm gun, centrally placed in turret, with MG co-axially mounted on right.

Sloping superstructure sides. No hull MG. Superstructure front and glacis plate combined in one clean slope.

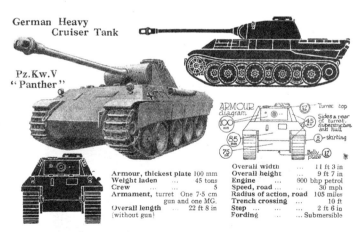

German Heavy
Cruiser Tank

Pz.Kw.V
" Panther "

ARMOUR diagram

Armour, thickest plate	100 mm
Weight laden	45 tons
Crew	5
Armament, turret	One 7·5 cm gun and one MG.
Overall length (without gun)	22 ft 8 in

Overall width	11 ft 3 in
Overall height	9 ft 7 in
Engine	600 bhp petrol
Speed, road	30 mph
Radius of action, road	105 miles
Trench crossing	10 ft
Step	2 ft 6 in
Fording	Submersible

Details of the Panzer V 'Panther' from *AFV Recognition, Part II, Enemy Turreted AFVs, Amendment 1*, of July 1943. The accuracy of information is high, but the term 'Cruiser' was unknown to the enemy – and potentially misleading. British 'Cruisers' tended to be relatively fast but less well armoured. The Panther was a near perfect balance of the 'armour triangle', being fast, well armed and well armoured. Teething troubles were its early weakness.

PRINCIPLES OF A.F.V. RECOGNITION

Important knowledge: the key features distinguishing a British Cruiser from the German Panzer in *Principles of AFV Recognition*.

A late model *Sturmgeschütz (StuG)* III assault gun pressed into US service. Based on the Panzer III chassis, the *StuG* was a useful low-silhouette vehicle, initially used for infantry support, but later also frequently deployed as a tank destroyer with a long 75 mm gun. With production of about 10,000 of all variants, this was the commonest type of tracked armoured fighting vehicle used by the German Army. The *StuG* had a crew of four, and a maximum armour thickness of 50 mm. Some late models were also fitted with additional side skirts. The top speed was approximately 40 kmph on roads.

CHAPTER 3

Notes on the German Army in War 1940

Produced by MI14 in December 1940, *Notes on the German Army in War* was supposed to be a summation of British knowledge to date and, despite the title, was actually a substantial, possibly over-ambitious, handbook of almost 400 pages replete with diagrams, tables and photographs. It radically updated the earlier work *Notes on the German Army* (1938) and superseded various of the short *Periodical Notes* pamphlets. Like the volumes produced on foreign forces just before and during the First World War, the new work was encyclopaedic in nature, thoroughly indexed and organised in thematic chapters. As might be expected, these covered organisation and administration, the various types of unit, small arms, support and anti-tank weapons, artillery, armour, engineers, signals and chemical warfare. There was also a briefer section on tactics and a description of uniform. Less obviously the volume had a short piece on the German airforce, and some remarks on police forces and political organisations.

The book also contained notes on captured equipment: part was verified intelligence, but part was deductive. Thus it was said with certainty that the Polish anti-tank rifle, known to the Germans as the *Tankbüchse,* 'was in use', but only that it was 'possible' that the Czech equivalents were being employed. Captured Polish and Czech tanks featured significantly, but French armour did not. This was perhaps surprising since a pamphlet entitled *French Armoured Vehicles Captured by the Germans*, attributed to MI3, had been produced as early as July 1940. This was supposed to be circulated down to platoon level to give 'all ranks an idea of the appearance of French Armoured Fighting Vehicles which might be used by the Germans'.

We now know that captured French armour saw significant use, albeit mainly on secondary fronts and as platforms for guns. Skoda and BMM continued to produce 'Czechoslovak'-designed tanks; these served with the German Army under the designations *Panzerkampfwagen* 35 (t) and 38 (t) respectively, the 38 (t) in particular forming the basis of a number of self-propelled guns and other equipment, some of which were still in use in 1945. Conversely, the Polish armour featured prominently in *Notes on the German Army in War* had existed only in relatively modest strength, some was of French or British design, and a significant portion had already been destroyed

The German soldier ca. 1940, from a private portrait. The *Feldbluse* (field jacket)
is of the type introduced in 1936 with dark green collar, and the 1935-type
steel helmet is adorned with two decals. On the wearer's right side the
shield was in the black, white and red colours of the state. On the left, seen
here, was depicted the army eagle in 'silver white', atop the swastika.

by the time the manual appeared. So it was that in a number of particulars the
picture presented was badly skewed from reality.

In theory an officer commanding a British formation could consult the
Notes and form swift estimates of German establishments when encountering
the enemy. Yet things were rarely so simple. For on the one hand the volume
was not as complete as it appeared at first glance, and on the other the enemy
was already in the habit of forming *Kampfgruppen* (battle groups made up
from parts of different formations, to perform specific operations). Sometimes
Notes on the German Army in War admitted its own shortcomings and
acknowledged being, despite solid appearance, a work in progress. In some
tables of information, blank spaces were left deliberately to indicate lack of data
or statements were qualified as beliefs.

An MG 34 machine gun, on exercise, c. 1939. The weapon is being used from
the steady Lafette tripod mounting. The gunner fires by means of a 'remote
trigger' and does not have to touch the gun itself while operating it.

In a few instances, facts were clearly and obviously wrong. The description
of the German steel helmet contained the observation that 'lugs are drilled on
either side of the helmet so that a face shield can be worn'. In reality, the steel
helmet introduced in 1935, unlike its First World War predecessor, had no
'lugs', merely air vents, and was not designed for use with a visor.

In another, more important example, the volume gives a description of a
'Panzer V/ VI' at the end of a list of enemy tanks and also presents two photos,
one each of a Panzer V and VI, with the latter apparently under construction or
repair. The reader might well be forgiven for thinking that these vehicles with a
'massive gun mounting' were a new phenomenon and followed the Panzer III
and IV designs chronologically. In point of fact, the strange Rheinmetall-built
beast only ever existed as a tiny trial batch made in 1934 to 1936. Just three
are known to have taken an active part in the Norwegian campaign, where their
performance was found wanting.

Indeed, it may be argued that the propaganda value of what the Germans
termed their *Neubaufahrzeug* ('new construction vehicle') was rather greater than
its combat worth. The vehicle had been shown to the press at the International
Automobile Exposition in Berlin in 1939, and was also pictured in Norway, where
the Germans appear to have taken little trouble to disguise its participation. British
intelligence swallowed its importance, not only accepting the *Neubaufahrzeug* as

two new tanks, Panzers V and VI, on account of different turret configurations, but exaggerating the weight up from 25 tons to 33 or 35 tons.

Given that a volume of the size of *Notes on the German Army in War* was not easy to consult rapidly, particularly on the move, it was issued with a duplicate set of the more important data for ready reference. The extracts we reproduce here cover the infantry, pages 15–37. The eighty-five original plates that accompanied *Notes on the German Army in War* focused primarily on small arms and support weapons, artillery, tanks and armoured cars, pontoons, rafts and assault boats, and uniform. These appear to have been taken principally from German sources and were generally adequate for purposes of identification, but not of sufficient clarity or resolution for reproduction in this book. Accordingly a smaller selection of period photographs, again substantially German in origin and covering some of the same subject matter, have been included here.

CHAPTER III

INFANTRY
1. General organization

The infantry arm is controlled by the Inspectorate of Infantry in the War Ministry. It consists of:—

(i)   Infantry regiments (normal type) (*Infanterie-Regimenter*), some of which include rifle (*Jäger*) battalions.

(ii) Motorised infantry regiments (*motorisierte Infanterie-Regimenter*) in motorised infantry divisions.

(iii) Mountain rifle regiments (*Gebirgsjäger-Regimenter*).

(iv) Motorised machine-gun battalions (*motorisierte Maschinengewehr-Bataillone*).

(v)   Motorised anti-aircraft machine-gun battalions (*Flugabwehr-Bataillone motorisiert*).

(vi) Fortress (*Festungs*) and frontier (*Grenz*) infantry regiments.

(vii) Certain S.S. and police regiments (*S.S. "Totenkopf" and "Verfügungs" Standarten* and *S.S. Polizei-Schützen-Regimenter*).

(viii) Positional units (*Stellungseinheiten*). (*See* Chapter I, para. 16 (*c*).)

(ix) Protective regiments (*Sicherungs-Regimenter*). (*See* Chapter I, para. 16 (*d*).)

The following units, which are under the Inspector of Mobile Troops (*Inspekteur der schnellen Truppen*) are included in this chapter for convenience:—

(i) Lorried infantry regiments in armoured divisions (*Schützen-Regimenter*).

(ii) Motor cyclist battalions (*Kradschützen-Bataillone*).

Parachute and air landing units (*Fallschirm- und Luftlandungseinheiten*) are described in Chapter XV.

2. Organization, strength and armament of an infantry regiment (normal type) (*Infanterie-Regiment*)

(*a*) *Organization*

(i) *Regiment.*—An infantry regiment consists of:—

Headquarters.

A signal section.

A motor-cyclist despatch rider section.

A mounted infantry platoon, consisting of headquarters and three sections.

A pioneer platoon. This has recently been added, and no details of its strength and organization are as yet known.

An infantry gun (13th) company (horse-drawn) of headquarters, signal section, three platoons each of two sections, each of the latter being armed with one 7·5-cm, (2·95-in.) light infantry gun; and one platoon of two sections, each of the latter being armed with one 15-cm. (5·91-in.) heavy infantry gun.[*]

[†]An anti-tank (14th) company. This unit, which is fully mechanized, consists of headquarters and four platoons. Each of the latter consists of three sections each armed with one 3·7-cm. (1·45-in.) anti-tank gun; and one light machine-gun

---

[*] It is believed that the Germans intend to give further support to their infantry by means of 7·5-cm. (2·95-in.) guns, mounted on converted light medium (Pz. Kw. III) tanks. These weapons are described as "assault guns" (*Sturmgeschütze*), and their role as that of highly mobile, close support artillery. It is claimed that the guns were successfully used on the Western Front, in the summer of 1940, but the scale of issue to units is not yet known.

[†] It is believed that the auti-tank company of an infantry regiment may be in process of reorganization into three antitank platoons each of four anti-tank guns. One anti-aircraft platoon of four 2-cm. (·79-in.) super-heavy anti-aircraft machineguns may also be added, but it is not yet established whether these machineguns have, in fact, been issued.

section; it is thought that the company no longer possesses a signal section.

A light infantry column (*see* para, 14 below).

Three battalions* (described in sub-para. (ii) below). (*See also* Appendices II and V.)

(ii) *Battalion.*—A battalion consists of headquarters, signal section, three rifle companies and one machine-gun company. These companies are numbered consecutively from 1 to 12 throughout the regiment, Nos. 4, 8 and 12 companies being machine-gun companies, (*See* Appendix V.)

(iii) *Rifle company.*—A rifle company consists of headquarters, an anti-tank rifle section armed with three anti-tank rifles, and three platoons. Each of the latter is divided into one light mortar section and four rifle sections; each rifle section includes one light machine-gun and one machine pistol. Platoon and company commanders also carry a machine pistol.

(iv) *Machine-gun company.*—A machine-gun company consists of headquarters, three machine-gun platoons and one mortar platoon. Each machine-gun platoon is divided into two machine-gun sections, each armed with two machine-guns. The mortar platoon consists of three mortar sections, each of two mortar sub-sections, each of one 8·1-cm. (3·16-in.) mortar.

(*See over for strength and armament.*)

3. Organization, strength and armament of a motorized infantry regiment (*motorisiertes Infanterie-Regiment*) in a motorized infantry division

(*a*) *Organization.*—The motorization of eighteen infantry regiments is now complete. Their organization is thought to be similar in general to that of a normal infantry regiment with the following differences:—

(i) The mounted infantry platoon is replaced by a 15th company for purposes of reconnaissance. This company has—

---

* A limited number of the normal infantry regiments contain a rifle (*Jäger*) battalion in the place of one of their normal battalions. These special rifle battalions are trained in ski-ing and mountain warfare. They contain a mountain gun company armed with four 7·5-cm. (2·95-in.) mountain guns. This company is an integral part of the battalion which is otherwise organized as a normal infantry battalion, but its transport is on a pack basis.

Six[*] light armoured cars.

Three motor-cyclist platoons.

(ii) The 13th (infantry gun) company is mechanised, the guns being drawn by semi-track tractors.

(b) *Strength.*—It is probable that the strength of a motorized infantry regiment will be approximately the same as that of an infantry regiment of the normal type (*see* para. 2 (*b*)). The number of vehicles in this unit is believed to be 334. Semi-track vehicles may eventually be introduced for transport of personnel.

(c) *Armament.*—This is the same as for an infantry regiment of normal type (*see* para. 2 (*c*)), with the additions mentioned in (*a*) (i) above.

4. Organization, strength and armament of a lorried infantry regiment (*Schützen-Regiment*) in an armoured division

(a) *Organization.*

(i) *Regiment.*—A lorried infantry regiment forms part of the lorried infantry brigade (*Schützen-Brigade*) in an armoured division.

It consists of headquarters (one platoon of four light and two heavy armoured cars and one motorized signal platoon), and two battalions.

(ii) *Battalion.*—Each battalion consists of headquarters, signal section and five companies, the latter being numbered consecutively from 1 to 10 throughout the regiment.

The five companies of the battalion are:—

One motor-cyclist company (No. 1).

Two rifle companies (Nos. 2 and 3).

One machine-gun company (No. 4). } Carried in lorries.

One "heavy" company (No. 5).

(iii) *Motor-cyclist company.*—The motor-cyclist company consists of headquarters, three platoons, each of three sections (each of the latter being armed with a machine-gun on a light mounting); and one platoon of two sections, each armed with two machine-guns on heavy mountings.

(iv) *Rifle company.*—Each rifle company consists of headquarters and three platoons, each of three sections. Each of the latter is divided into a rifle sub-section and a subsection armed with a

---

[*] It is believed that this number may be increased.

Transhipment of a *Neubaufahrzeug* ('new construction vehicle') during transport to Norway, 1940, from the album of Austrian Ludwig Pöltl, an NCO with Mountain Engineer Battalion 83. Lax security and propaganda could exaggerate the apparent importance of equipment.

machine-gun on a light mounting. Each section is carried in a Krupp six-wheeled lorry. The machine-guns are in some cases mounted on a narrow platform behind the driving seat.

(v) *Machine-gun company.*—The machine-gun company consists of headquarters, signal section and three platoons. Each platoon is divided into two machine-gun sections, each of two sub-sections, each armed with one machine-gun on heavy mounting.

(vi) *Heavy company.*—The heavy company consists of:

An anti-tank platoon organized in the same way as the equivalent unit in the anti-tank company of an infantry regiment of the normal type (*see* para. 2 (*a*) (i)).

A close support platoon which is believed to consist of four sections each armed with one 7·5-cm. (2·95-in.) infantry gun. These guns have pneumatic-tyred carriages and are towed behind six-wheeled lorries, as are also the ammunition trailers.

An engineer platoon of three sections, each armed with one machine-gun on a light mounting.

(b) Approximate Strengths.*

	Officers.	Other ranks.	Motor-cycles.	M.C. combinations.	2-seater cars.	4-seater cars.	6-wheeled lorries or motor limbers.	Vans.	Field cookers on lorries.	Light lorries for repairs, supplies, etc.	Heavy lorries for repairs.	3-ton bridging lorries.	Pontoon trailers.	Ammunition trailers.
Regt.	1	—	—	—	—	—	—	—	—	—	—	6	6	4
Regt. Sig. Sec.	—	—	—	—	—	—	—	—	—	—	—	—	—	—
Bn.	1	—	—	—	—	—	—	—	—	—	1	3	3	2
Bn. Sig. Sec.	—	—	—	—	—	—	—	—	—	—	—	—	—	—
M.C. Coy.	4	152	8	41	—	5	—	—	5	10	—	—	—	—
M.C. Pl. with L.M.Gs.	1	34	2	9	—	1	—	—	1	1	—	—	—	—
M.C. Pl. with Hy. M.Gs.	—	18	—	10	—	—	—	—	—	—	—	—	—	—
Rifle Coy.	4	174	1	1	—	1	6	—	5	—	—	—	—	—
Rifle Pl.	1	45	—	—	—	—	—	—	—	—	—	—	—	—
M.G. Coy.	4	121	—	1	—	—	—	1	5	—	—	—	—	—
M.G. Pl.	1	31	—	—	—	—	—	1	5	—	—	—	—	—
Hy. Coy.	4	30	3	1	—	1	—	—	1	6	—	—	—	—
A. Tk. Pl.	1	32	1	1	—	1	3	—	—	1	—	—	—	2
Cl. Sup. Pl.	1	—	1	1	—	1	4	—	—	—	—	—	—	—
Eng. Pl.	1	—	—	—	—	—	—	—	—	—	—	3	3	—

*In cases where the strength of personnel and/or vehicles is not known, columns have been left blank.

(c) *Armament.*

	Dual purpose M.Gs. on light mounting.	Dual purpose M.Gs. on heavy mounting.	3·7-cm. (1·45-in.) A. Tk. guns.	7·5-cm. (2·95-in.) Inf. guns.	2-cm (·79-in.) Super-heavy M.Gs.
Regt.	68	32	6	8	2
H.Q.	6	—	—	—	2
Bn.	31	16	3	4	—
M.C. Coy.	9	4	—	—	—
Rifle Coy.	9	—	—	—	—
M.G. Coy.	—	12	—	—	...
Hy. Coy.	4	—	3	4	—

5. Organization, strength and armament of a mountain rifle regiment (*Gebirgsjäger-Regiment*)

(a) *Organization and strength,*—Mountain rifle regiments are primarily regarded as Alpine troops and are equipped as such. Full details regarding their organization and strength are not available, but they are believed to be organized in the same way as normal infantry regiments (*see* para, 2), except that their transport is almost entirely on a pack basis.

(b) *Armament.*—The only difference in armament between a mountain rifle regiment and an infantry regiment of the normal type (*see* para. 2 (c)) lies in the equipment of the 13th Company, which in the case of the former unit is believed to consist of eight 7·5-cm. (2·95-in.) mountain guns.

6. Organization, strength and armament of a motor-cyclist battalion (*Kradschützen-Bataillon*)

(a) *Organization.*

    (i) *Battalion.*—A motor-cyclist battalion forms part of the lorried infantry brigade in an armoured division. It consists of headquarters (one platoon of four light and two heavy armoured cars, and one motorized signal platoon), three motor-cyclist rifle companies, one motor-cyclist machine-gun company and one heavy company.

(b) Approximate Strengths.

	H.T.					M.T.							
	Others.	Other ranks.	1 or 2-horsed wagons.	4-horsed wagons.	2-horsed field kitchens.	Solo motor-cycles.	M.C. combinations.	2-seater cars.	4-seater cross-country cars.	Motor limbers.	Field cookers on lorries.	Lorry workshop.	Lorries (light or medium).
Regt.	95	2,993	—	—	—	—	—	—	—	—	—	—	—
Regtl. H.Q.	6	28	1	—	1	4	2	—	—	—	—	—	2
Regtl Sig. Sec.	1	48	3	—	—	—	—	—	—	—	—	—	1
M.C.D.R. Sec.	—	—	—	—	—	—	—	—	—	—	—	—	—
M.I. Pl.	1	31	1	—	—	—	—	—	—	—	—	—	—
Pioneer Platoon	—	—	—	—	—	—	—	—	—	—	—	—	—
Inf. Gun Coy.	5	185	3	11*	1	—	—	—	—	—	—	—	—
Sig. Sec. in Inf. Gun Coy.	—	23	1	—	—	—	—	—	—	—	—	—	—
Lt. Pl. in Inf. Gun Coy.	1	32	—	2	—	—	—	—	—	—	—	—	1
Hy. Pl. in Inf. Gun Coy.	1	34	—	2	—	—	—	—	—	—	—	—	—
A.Tk. Coy.	5	165	—	—	—	16	6	—	11	25	1	—	5
A.Tk. Coy. Sig. Sec.†	—	22	—	—	—	—	—	—	6	—	—	—	—
H.Q. Pl.	1	11	—	—	—	4	2	—	1	—	—	—	—
A.Tk. Pl.	1	34	—	—	—	3	1	—	1	6	—	—	—
Lt. Inf. Col.	2	97	39	—	5	1	1	—	—	—	1	1	6
Bn.	25	813	40	—	5	4	1	—	2	—	—	—	6
Bn. H.Q.	6	15	5	—	—	4	1	—	2	—	—	—	—
Bn. Tpt.	1	26	1	—	1	—	—	—	—	—	—	—	3
Bn. Sig. Sec.	1	38	5	—	—	—	—	—	—	—	—	—	1
Rifle Coy.	4	183	1	—	1	—	—	—	—	—	—	—	—
Rifle Pl.	1	48	—	—	—	—	—	—	—	—	—	—	—
A.Tk. Rifle Sec. in Rifle Coy.	—	7	2	—	—	—	—	—	—	—	—	—	—
M.G. Coy.	5	185	19	—	1	—	—	—	—	—	—	—	—
M.G. Pl.	1	31		—	—	—	—	—	—	—	—	—	—
Mortar Pl.	1	64		—	—	—	—	—	—	—	—	—	—
M.G. Coy. H.Q.	1	12		—	—	—	—	—	—	—	—	—	—
M.G. Coy. Tpt.	—	16		—	—	—	—	—	—	—	—	—	—

* This figure does not include six four-horsed and two six-horsed gun limbers.
† It is possible that the A.Tk. company no longer has a signal section.
(In cases where the strength of personnel and/or vehicles is not known, columns have been left blank.)

(c) Armament.

	L.M.Gs.†	Hy. M.Gs.†	2-cm. (·79-in.) A. Tk. rifles.	3·7-cm. (1·45-in.) A. Tk. guns.	5-cm. (2-in.) mortars.	8·1-cm. (3·16-in.) mortars.	7·5-cm. (2·95-in.) light infantry guns.	15-cm. (5·91-in.) heavy infantry guns.	Machine pistols.
Regt. ...	112	36	27	12	27	18	6*	2*	144
Inf. Gun Coy.							6	2	
Lt. Inf. Gun Pl.							2		
Hy. Inf. Gun Pl.								2	
A. Tk. Coy.	4			12					
A. Tk. Pl.	1			3					
Bn. ...	36	12	9		9	6			48
Rifle Coy.	12		3		3				16
Rifle Pl.	4				1				5
A. Tk. Rifle Sec. in Rifle Coy.			3						
M.G. Coy.		12				6			
M.G. Pl.		4							
Mortar Pl. in M.G. Coy.						6			

* It is believed that the number of light infantry guns in a regiment is to be reduced to four and it is possible that the number of heavy infantry guns will be increased to four.

† Eventually both the light and the heavy machine-gun will be replaced by the dual purpose weapon (M.G. 34) and it is believed that the change has already been made in all active units and in the majority of units formed on and since mobilisation.

(ii) *Motor-cyclist rifle company.*—A motor-cyclist rifle company is organized in three platoons, each of three sections, each of the latter having one machine-gun on a light mounting; and one machine-gun platoon with two machine-guns on heavy mountings.

(iii) *Motor-cyclist machine-gun company.*—A motor-cyclist machine-gun company consists of headquarters and three platoons, each of two machine-gun sections. Each of the latter is provided with two machine-guns on heavy mountings.

(iv) *Heavy company.*—The heavy company is organized in the same way as the equivalent unit in a lorried infantry regiment in an armoured division (*see* para. 4 (*a*) (vi)).

(*See opposite for strength and armament.*)

(*c*) *Armament.*

	Dual purpose M.Gs. on light mounting.	Dual purpose M.Gs. on heavy mounting.	3·7-cm. (1·45-in.) A.Tk. guns.	7·5-cm. (2·95-in.) Inf. guns.	2-cm. (·79-in.) Super heavy M.Gs.
M.C. Bn.	37	18	3	4	2
Bn. H.Q.	6	—	—	—	2
M.C.Rifle Coy.	9	2	—	—	—
M.C. M.G. Coy.	—	12	—	—	—
Hy. Coy.	4	—	3	4	—

(b) Strengths.*

Unit	Officers	Other ranks	Motor-cycles	M.C. combinations	2-seater cars	4-seater cars	6-wheeled lorries or motor limbers for drawing guns	Field cooker on light lorry	Light lorries for supplies, repairs, etc.	Heavy lorries for repairs	3-ton bridging lorries	Pontoon trailers	Ammunition trailers
M.C. Bn.	—	—	—	—	—	—	—	—	—	1	3	3	2
Sig. Sec.	1	—	—	—	—	—	—	—	—	—	—	—	—
M.C. Rifle Coy.	4	174	8	41	—	5	—	1	10	—	—	—	—
Rifle Pl. in Rifle Coy.	1	45	2	9	—	1	—	—	1	—	—	—	—
A.Tk. Rifle Sec. in Rifle Coy.	—	7	—	—	1	—	—	—	—	—	—	—	—
M.C. M.G. Coy.	4	—	—	—	—	—	—	1	—	—	—	—	—
M.C. M.G. Pl.	1	—	—	—	—	—	—	—	—	—	—	—	—
Hy. Coy.	4	30	3	1	—	1	7	1	6	—	3	3	2
A.Tk. Pl.	1	32	1	1	—	1	3	—	1	—	—	—	2
Cl. Sup. Pl.	1	—	—	—	—	—	4	—	—	—	—	—	—
Eng. Pl.	1	—	—	—	—	—	—	—	—	—	3	3	—

* In cases where the strength of personnel and/or vehicles is not known, columns have been left blank.

7 Organization, strength and armament of a motorized machine-gun battalion (motorisiertes *Maschinen-gewehr-Bataillon*).

(*a*) *Organization.*

    (i) *Battalion.*—A motorized machine-gun battalion consists at present of headquarters, headquarters motor-cyclist platoon, signal section, three machine-gun companies and one anti-tank company. This organization cannot, however, be regarded as being permanent, and the unit may eventually include engineers, armoured cars and infantry guns.

    (ii) *Headquarters motor-cyclist platoon.*—Details of this unit, which is used for reconnaissance and inter-communication, are not known. It is armed with three or four machine-guns on light mountings.

    (iii) *Machine-gun company.*—A machine-gun company consists of four platoons each armed with four machine-guns. Three of these platoons, armed with dual purpose machine-guns on heavy mountings, are carried in light six-wheeled lorries, and the fourth, armed with dual purpose machine-guns on light mountings, on motor-cycles and sidecars.

    (iv) *Anti-tank company.*—The anti-tank company is, it is believed, organized in the same way as the equivalent unit in an infantry regiment of normal type (*see* para. 2 (*a*)).

Some German hardware was already familiar to the Allies. The 08/15 light machine gun, seen here, was a standard of the First World War. About 130,000 of this water-cooled model firing from fabric belts were made by 1918. The easiest way to examine one was in military museums in Britain and the US.

An informal group portrait of an MG 13 machine-gun team. Developed after
the First World War, the MG 13 light machine gun was still in limited use
in 1939. The distinctive curved bags are pouches for the magazines.

(*b*) *Strength.*[*]

	Officers.	Other ranks.	Motor-cycles, medium, solo.	Motor-cycles, heavy, with sidecars.	Passenger cars.
M.G. Bn.	26	964	87	70	181
H.Q. incl. M.G. Pl.	6	104	7	10	33
M.G. Coy.	5	234	22	18	38
A.Tk. Coy.	5	158	14	6	34

(*c*) *Armament.*

	Dual purpose machine-guns on light mounting.	Dual purpose machine-guns on heavy mounting.	3·7-cm. (1·45-in.) A.Tk. guns.
Bn.	? 20	36	12
H.Q. M.C. Pl.	? 4	—	—
M.G. Coy.	4	12	—
A.Tk. Coy.	4	—	12

---

[*] First and second line transport *not* included.

8. Frontier infantry regiment
(Grenz-Infanterie-Regiment)

The organization, strength and armament of a frontier infantry regiment are the same as those of ordinary infantry regiments.

9. Organization of S.S. formations
(see also Chapter XII, para. 4)

Certain S.S. formations are permanently embodied, and fully trained for military service. They may be divided into two categories:—

(a) The S.S. (*Verfügungstruppen*) of which there are the following regiments—"Leibstandarte Adolf. Hitler," "Standarte Germania," "Standarte Deutschland" and "Standarte Der Führer." The last three have been combined into the "S.S. Verfügungsdivision," which is organized, armed and equipped as an ordinary motorized division.

(b) S.S. (*Totenkopf*) units. An "S.S. Totenkopf-Division" is known to have been formed. It is organized, armed and equipped as an ordinary motorized division.

10. Parachute and air-landing units

The Air Force has now taken over all responsibility for the provision and training of men employed in parachute units, and they are now exclusively Air Force personnel.

For further details of parachute and air-landing troops *see* Chapter XV.

11. Organization, strength and armament of a motorized anti-aircraft machine-gun battalion. (Flugabwehr-Bataillon motorisiert)*

(a) *Organization.*

(i) *Battalion.*—A motorized anti-aircraft machine-gun battalion consists of headquarters and three machine-gun companies.

---

*This was previously known as "Maschinengewehr-Bataillon schwer motorisiert."

To date a number of anti-aircraft machine-gun battalions have been identified and it is believed that they will be provided on the scale of one per division, though it is possible that the present allotment per division may he only one company. Their primary role is A.A. defence, with A.Tk. defence as their secondary role.

(ii) *Machine gun company.*—Each company has three platoons, each of two sections. Each section is armed with two 2-cm, (·79-in.) super-heavy machine-guns (*überschwere M.G.*).

(b) *Strength.*—No details are yet known.

(c) *Armament.*—The battalion has thirty-six 2-cm. (·79-in.) super-heavy M.Gs. (*überschwere M.G.*). These weapons can be used against tanks as well as in their primary role against aircraft.

(d) *Searchlight detachment.*—The battalion is believed to have a searchlight detachment with searchlights of the light 60-cm. (1 ft. 11 1/2 in.) type.

12. Regimental specialists

(a) *Assault detachments* (*Stosstrupps*).

(i) *Personnel.*—These detachments of infantry, specially trained as raiding parties for a particular operation, are composed of carefully selected volunteers from within their company. A typical party consists of one officer, four N.C.Os. and approximately forty other ranks.

(ii) *Arms and equipment.*—All personnel carry respirators if gas is anticipated and each man carries, in addition to his rifle and bayonet, four hand grenades, two in his belt and two in his boots. Each of the four N.C.Os, is armed with a machine pistol. It is believed that three heavy machine guns are placed at the disposal of the detachment by the battalion and two light machine guns are made available by the company. The officer has under his charge two messenger dogs on leads. He carries a Verey pistol, whistle and pocket torch. Other equipment includes wire cutters, gloves, daggers, spades and tent canvas for the removal of dead and wounded men and captured material.

Where the operation demands the destruction of a particular objective, engineers, to the number of about sixteen, may be added to the detachment. They carry pole charges, smoke grenades and flame throwers. All personnel wear a distinctive sign which can be easily seen. (*See also* Chapter VIII, para. 16.)

(b) *Signallers.*—All signallers are trained regimentally. The strengths of the various signal sections, so far as these are known, are given in the paragraphs dealing with the various types of infantry units. Their equipment is shown in para. 16 (*e*).

(c)   *Pioneers.*—Approximately one section of each company in an infantry regiment is trained in pioneer duties n the field. Sections can be formed into a battalion pioneer platoon as required, but they do not handle mines or explosives.

(d)   *M.T. specialists.*—All drivers of motor transport in infantry units are trained as mechanics and can carry out minor repairs. Mechanics with more specialized knowledge are carried on the repair lorries which accompany the head-quarters of companies, battalions and regiments

(e)   *Other specialists.*—All infantry units down to companies include armourers and anti-gas specialists, and battalions include tailors and cobblers.

13. Numbering of units

All infantry regiments (including motorized and frontier infantry, and mountain rifle regiments) are numbered in one continuous series. Except for the mountain rifle (*Gebirgsjäger*) regiments and the rifle battalions included in certain normal infantry regiments they wear white numerals. These mountain rifle units wear green numerals.

Lorried infantry (*Schützen*) regiments and motor-cyclist (*Kradschützen*) battalions are numbered in two different series. When part of an armoured division, both wear pink numerals.

14. Regimental transport

Details, so far as these are known regarding the types and numbers of vehicles in regimental first line transport, are included in the paragraphs dealing with the strength of the various types of infantry units.

First line transport is divided into actual vehicles required for fighting (*Kampffahrzeuge*), battle transport (*Gefechtstross*) which includes unit cookers baggage transport (*Gepäcktross*) and supply transport (*Verpflegungstross*). The horse portion of the latter carries the current day's rations; the mechanized portion carries the rations for the next day which it has collected from the divisional refilling point.

The second line transport of infantry regiments consists of a light infantry column (*leichte Infanteriekolonne*). It consists of thirty-nine two-horsed wagons with a total capacity of 19 tons. It is organized in a headquarters, an ammunition section and a stores section, and carries ammunition and all stores, except rations, from the divisional refilling point to units.

15. Ammunition supply

The system of ammunition supply is the same as that in the British army, *i.e.,* systematic replacement of ammunition as it is expended. Ammunition comes up from the M.T. echelons in rear to the light infantry column and thence by way of battalion and company reserves to the individual rifleman or machine-gunner. The following table shows the scale of issue of ammunition:—

Weapon.	On the man or with the gun.	Company and battalion reserve.	Remarks.
Rifle	90 rounds per man in rifle coys. 45 rounds per man in other coys.	40 rounds per man.	
Machine pistol	6 magazines each holding 32 rounds, in ammunition pouches.		
Light machine-gun.	3,100 rounds per gun divided between the gun team and the company and battalion reserve.		The L.M.Gs. in the A.Tk. coy. each have 1,000 rounds.
Heavy machine-gun.	5,250 rounds per gun divided between the company limbers and the battalion reserve.		
Revolver	32 rounds per man.	Not known.	
Grenade	Not known.	Not known.	

16. EQUIPMENT

(*a*) *Personal.*—The weight carried by the infantryman has been considerably reduced as his pack is now carried on a limber.

(*b*) *Steel Helmet.* (*See* Chapter XIII, para 1 (*a*).)

(*c*) *Respirator.* (*See* Chapter X, para. 3 (*b*) (i).)

(*d*) *Gas Cape.* (*See* Chapter X, para. 3 (*b*) (ii).)

(*e*) *Signal Equipment.*—The telephone and wireless equipment carried by an infantry regiment of normal type is given below. It is probable that approximately the same amount is carried by a motorized infantry regiment and a mountain rifle regiment.

	Medium cable (miles).	Light cable (miles).	Exchanges.	Field Telephones.	Pack Wireless Sets.	Medium Lamps.	Small Lamps.	Messenger Dogs.
Regt. Sig. Sec.	9	5	4	12	4	2	—	
Inf. Gun Coy.		8		12				
A.Tk. Coy.	—	2 1/2	—	4	5	—	—	—
Rifle Bn. Sig. Sec.	—	5	4	6	4	4	—	3
Rifle Coy.	—	—	—	—	—	—	2	—
M.G. Coy.	—	8	4	6	—	—	2	—
M.C. Bn.	5	5	1?	5	2			

Details of the above equipment are given in Chapter IX.

It is not at present known what telephone and wireless equipment is carried by a lorried infantry regiment in an armoured division, a motor-cyclist battalion, a motorized machine-gun battalion, a frontier battalion, or a fortress battalion.

In addition to telephone and wireless equipment, the following signal equipment is also provided:—

(i) White strips for communication with aircraft, with a red back for use on snow. (*See* Appendix XLIX.)

(ii) Flares to show the positions of the leading infantry.

(iii) Verey pistols with red, white, green, yellow and other coloured lights.

(iv) Red and white signalling discs.

All the above are used in accordance with recognized codes. (i) and (ii) are issued down to and including headquarters of companies; (iii) and (iv) down to and including headquarters of platoons.

(f) *Tools.*—Every infantryman carries an entrenching tool of some kind. Details regarding the reserves of tools carried on the company, battalion and regimental vehicles are not at present known.

(g) *Rangefinder.*—This is of the "inverted image" type and is similar to that in use in machine-gun battalions in the British army.

(h) *Bivouacs.*—Each infantryman has a camouflaged coloured waterproof sheet complete with poles, pegs and cords. A number of these sheets can be fastened together to make improvised shelters or tents.

(i)   *Engineer Equipment.*—Six large and six small pneumatic boats are carried in the vehicles of the engineer platoon of a motor-cyclist battalion and of each battalion of a lorried infantry regiment in an armoured division.

Pneumatic boats are also carried by other infantry units, but the number and types are not at present known.

(j)   *Anti-A.F.V. Equipment.*—Each anti-tank platoon carries twelve rolls of concertina wire for road blocks.

APPENDIX III

APPROXIMATE STRENGTH IN PERSONNEL AND VEHICLES (H.T. AND M.T.) OF AN INFANTRY DIVISION

	Officers.	O.Rs.	Motor Cycles.	Motor Vehicles.	Horsed Transport.	Horses.
Divisional H.Q.	12	140	12	26		20
Divisional Recce. Unit	15	560	30	30	3	213
Divisional Signals	15	456	28	102	7	56
Divisional Inf. H.Q.	4					
Divisional Infantry	285	8,997	135	210	612	1,440
Divisional Artillery H.Q.						
Divisional Artillery	89	2,156	12	23	178	1,785
Divisional Anti-Tank Bn.	20	770	80	170	—	—
Divisional Engineer Bn.	20	667	26	53	19	52
Divisional Medical Coy.	15	463	17	86		50
Divisional Veterinary Coy.	6	228	—	—		188
Services (units of which strength known)	16	515	16	340		—
Total	497	14,952	356	1,040	819	3,804
* Motorized A.A.M.G. Bn.	21	800	137	147	—	—

* It has not yet been definitely established whether it is intended to include one of these units in each division, or whether they are to remain G.H.Q. troops.

APPENDIX IV

FIRE POWER OF AN INFANTRY DIVISION

	Div. Recce. Unit.	Div. Inf.	Div. Arty.	Mot. M.G. Bn. (A.A.).[1]	Div. A.Tk. Bn.	Div. Eng. Bn.	Total.
Machine pistols (excl. those in armoured cars)	—	432	—	—	—	—	432
Machine guns, light mounting	24	336	24	—	18	28	430
Machine guns, heavy mounting	8	108	—	—	—	—	116
2-cm. (·79-in.) A.Tk. rifles	—	81	—	—	—	—	81
2-cm. (·79-in.) A.A. and A.Tk. guns	—	12[3]	24	36	12	—	84
3·7-cm. (1·45-in.) A. Tk. guns	3	36	—	—	36	—	75
5-cm. (2-in.) mortars	3	81	—	—	—	—	84
8·1-cm, (3·16-in.) mortars (*see* note [2])	3[2]	54	—	—	—	—	57
7·5-cm. (2·95-in.) infantry guns	2	18	—	—	—	—	20
15-cm. (5·91-in.) infantry guns	—	6	—	—	—	—	6
10·5-cm. (4·14-in.) gun-howitzers	—	—	36	—	—	—	36
10·5-cm. (4·14-in.) guns	—	—	4	—	—	—	4
15-cm. (5·91-in.) howitzers	—	—	8	—	—	—	8

Notes.—[1] It has not yet been definitely established whether it is intended to include one of these units por division, or whether they are to remain G.H.Q. troops. The 2-cm. (·79-in.) super-heavy A.A.M.G.s can also be used for an anti-tank role.

[2] The existence of three 8·1-cm. (3·16-in.) mortars in the div. recce. unit is not confirmed.

[3] The issue of four 2 cm. (·79-in.) A.A. and A.Tk. guns to the A.Tk. coy. of the infantry regiment has not yet been confirmed.

The *Granatwerfer* 36.5 cm light mortar was standard issue to the
German Infantry Platoon for much of the war. A captured example was
tested in the UK in 1941. The resulting report remarked that it was 'well
constructed and easy to operate' though possibly over-engineered.

CHAPTER 4
WAR: The German Army, May 1942

WAR was a journal of the British Army Bureau of Current Affairs (ABCA), an organisation dedicated to education and supporting the morale of British servicemen. The little pamphlet was usually sixteen pages long and publication ran from 1941 to 1945, with a French-language version for French-Canadian troops and extra editions over and above the normal fortnightly production during the last months of its existence. *WAR* was intended as an adjunct to the lecturing work of the ABCA, as explained by WE Williams, secretary of the British Institute of Adult Education and head of ABCA in 1942:

> The aim of A.B.C.A., as its name implies, is to make the average private understand the world he is living in, the cause he is fighting for and the nations he is fighting side by side with. The method is lectures, not by eminent experts from outside, but by the regimental officers, each officer as a rule dealing with his own platoon, who themselves rely in the first instance on two admirable bulletins, *War* and *Current Affairs*, prepared by the War Office for this specific purpose. Units are not compelled to arrange these lectures, but something between 60 per cent. and 80 per cent. do arrange them, and the general conclusion reached is that the average standard of the talks is higher than might have been expected, that the men on the whole decidedly appreciate the innovation, and that the talk that goes best is one that slides off naturally into a general discussion, with the officer evolving from a lecturer into a chairman.

This may have appeared non-controversial. However, in practice, soldiers who knew more were not only better-informed and motivated but also more equipped to question. The ABCA was already viewed in conservative circles as left-leaning, and 'Bill' Williams, editor in chief at Penguin Books at the outbreak of war in 1939, was dedicated to both life-long learning and the notion of cultural democracy. Matters came to a head in parliament in 1943 when a summary of the *Beveridge Report* was prepared for circulation by the ABCA and then withdrawn. It was becoming increasingly clear that there was public appetite to fight the war not just against Nazism but for the creation of a better world. In these and other respects *WAR* bears interesting comparison with the US film series *Why We Fight,* directed by Frank Capra, which included animated segments by the Disney Studios. The objectives may have been similar, but the execution and apparent results would be dramatically different.

Knowledge of Allies and enemies was a running theme in both *Why We Fight* and *WAR*. In the case of *WAR*, there were snippets entitled 'facts for fighting men' scattered through many of its editions and in 1942, in particular, a number of issues were devoted primarily to German matters. For example, in no. 15, of April 1942, 'The mind of a Nazi' was the point in question, but it is no. 17's 'The German Army', of May 1942, that interests us here. As well as the main feature on the German Army reproduced here, this issue also contained an article on tanks in the Red Army. Shorter notes addressed the long-range artillery duel across the Channel, Americans in Burma, the German birth rate, shipping, an Italian soldier apprehended in drag by 'an agent of the secret police', and the spread of typhus.

'The German Army' is interesting in that while the message is clear that the enemy can, and will, be beaten, this will not be easy since Germany has a good educational system and a long military tradition, with troops well trained and disciplined, crafty, tough and possessing tactical skills. This is perhaps both surprising and surprisingly realistic: *WAR* does not want the British soldier being misled into thinking that his enemy is a stupid automaton or a pushover. It does want to educate the reader in the strengths and weaknesses of his enemy.

THE MAN WE'RE UP AGAINST
The German Army

This is the first of a series of articles which will appear in WAR from time to time under the general title. "The Man We're Up Against." Here is presented an authentic picture of the German Army, its background and the men who serve in it—written by a British senior officer who had personal contact with the German Army in the years immediately preceding the war.

FREDERICK THE GREAT inherited from his father Frederick William, known as the "soldier King," a standing army fourth in numbers and probably first in training and discipline of the continental armies of the day—a force famous for the exactness of its drill at a time when steadiness of drill in the mass was the first tactical requisite on the battle-field; and the earliest army ever trained to march in step. This force, used by Frederick in unscrupulous and desperate adventures, which exhausted but also inspired his country, laid the foundations of modern Prussia.

When at Frederick's death the directing genius failed, the whole organism decayed; and the Prussian power was soon afterwards completely overwhelmed by the revolutionary armies of Napoleon. The six years of subjection to France which followed produced a truly national reaction. It was a citizen army which, hurriedly improvised in 1813, helped to bring Napoleon down; and the reformers, who now for the first time introduced universal military service, valued this militia spirit highly, and did all they could to encourage it.

But that spirit, associated with the liberalism of the time, perished in the political conflicts of the first part of the nineteenth century. By the fifties the army was once more a professional preserve, officered almost entirely by the aristocracy and tending to stagnation; conscientious, but thoroughly dull. No one would have expected that it was soon to upset the whole balance of Europe.

They Learned Lessons

The Franco-Austrian War of 1859 gave the Prussian Government the opportunity of discovering, without themselves being put to the test, the shortcomings of their forces. The occasion was not missed, and produced the men to grasp it—Bismarck, the statesman, who forced through his army reforms in the face of Parliament, and Moltke, the creator of the Great General Staff. Between them they created the army which to 1866, in a campaign of six weeks, set Prussia once for all in Austria's place as the chief German power; and which in 1870-1 destroyed the French Second Empire and reduced France to a decided military inferiority.

They had good material to work on. The high standard of education in Prussia earned for the battle of Königgrätz, which decided the Austrian war, the name of the "schoolmaster's victory." The army, greatly enlarged by Bismarck, was armed with the new "needle-gun" or breech-loading rifle, which increased greatly the fire power of the infantry; and the General Staff under Moltke was the first to realise the immense changes in strategic tempo made possible, since the Napoleonic Wars, by the introduction of railways and telegraphs.

The Soldier's Prestige

Bismarck, by not going too far, was able to hold what he had won. No sudden downfall or revenge of fate undid his victories. The spirit of Prussian militarism, feeding on its own success, grew almost unchallenged; and all the while Germany was undergoing the far-reaching and rapid industrialisation which was to enable her to sustain war so well upon the modern scale.

Nothing could be stronger proof of the military instincts of the German people than their ability, through a whole generation of unbroken peace, to maintain the condition of their army. Twenty or thirty years of rest after victory have often proved enough for a tested military system to fall into disrepair. But the German Army was never readier for war, nor its efficiency higher, than in 1914. The General Staff did its work with thorough care; and the military enjoyed an unequalled social prestige.

The story of Hauptmann von Köpenick belongs most truly to this period. This little saddler for a hoax disguised himself as a Prussian officer, fell in a squad of soldiers, marched them to the station, commandeered transport to a neighbouring town and arrested the Mayor, all without anyone's daring to stop him. This story is not a satire, it is true.

Deadlock in the Trenches

The Great War of 1914–18 produced a sequence of brilliant German professional successes on the Eastern front. Serbia, Rumania and Russia were overrun or shattered. But in the west, after the initial blow had failed, the military science of both sides came to a deadlock in the trenches, which only the combined pressure of land and sea power was able to resolve. When it seemed that the Allied offensives could make no head against Germany on land, that pressure drove Ludendorff in turn to stake everything on a great offensive of his own; and when this failed, and then recoiled, he was beaten. The Allied counter-attacks drove him back with increasing speed from the Marne and Amiens to the Belgian frontier. The Balkan front collapsed, and his fate was decided. At the end of September, 1918, Ludendorff himself gave orders to seek an Armistice. The German Army had been decisively beaten in the field.

The Treaty of Versailles abolished conscription in Germany, and allowed the new republic a long service army of only 100,000 men, without tanks, aircraft or heavy artillery. The stages by which these limits were first evaded and then repudiated are well known.

The 100,000 Army

In March, 1935, Hitler re-introduced universal military service, and next year raised the army to 36 divisions, and at the same time the great rearmament began. He had at his disposal an obedient people, a well-equipped though rather rusty industry, and four or five years; and he made full use of them all. The members of the "100,000 Army" became officers and N.C.Os. in Hitler's new army. He had, too, a clear field for the standardisation of military equipment which is characteristic of his armies to-day. He commenced forming the Panzer divisions which were to prove so formidable later.

The great German General Staff was revived in all its ancient glory. A combined staff containing representatives of all three services was set up in Berlin. The task of this staff, under its chief, was to dictate the nation's military policy, both strategic and economic, for all these services. It contained a "War Economics" section, which assisted at its labours. While this central staff dictated policy, the Ministries of War, Navy and Air were responsible for all the executive work resulting from that policy. No one service was predominant, although it was tacitly admitted that for Germany, a continental nation, the army was the most important thing, and that it would be the army which in the end would win a war for Germany.

Mobilisation System

For the purpose of recruiting and military administration, Germany, now including Austria, the Protectorate, Danzig and Posen, is divided into 18 military administrative areas, and these again into a hierarchy of small units. In peace-time each area furnished one corps. On mobilisation these corps took the field under their area commanders, and the area remained under the administrative command of a deputy G.O.C., the depots being occupied by depot units of the "Ersatzheer," or Reserve Army. Such, at least, is the basis of the system; though its regularity has now been modified by the grouping of certain reserve units into reserve divisions serving as low category formations in the Field Army. It is to these units that the recruit is first drafted.

But the working of conscription in Nazi Germany cannot be understood without a view of the pre-military training to which German youth has been subjected. From the age of 12, German boys have, since 1933, been drilled in youth organisations only nominally voluntary, and all directed to the upbringing of Nazi soldiers. Two things have been taught them—first, a soldierly ability to live hard: second, an unquestioning respect for authority. This combination provides the army with material that is, within its limitations, formidable.

Besides membership of these organisations every youth has also, or had, after enlistment but before his military service, to undergo six months' labour service on land reclamation and other similar undertakings. This labour service, though now sometimes omitted, has been a most important Nazi institution. Every advantage has been taken of the opportunities which the system afforded for relentless Nazification. Each evening has been spent in the organised absorbing of propaganda. Drill, harangues and community singing have filled every minute of spare time. And yet the most sinister thing perhaps is not that German youth should be subjected to this process, but that they should enjoy it.

It follows that when the peace-time conscript finally arrived at his two years' military service, it appeared more like a promotion than an interruption of his career. Life was more interesting and probably more comfortable than what he had recently known. The lessons of discipline had already been learnt; and he passed at once to the acquiring of that professional competence which marks the German soldier.

Hitler's Knowledge

Hitler's absorbing interest has been his Army, much more than his Air Force or Navy. He has himself considerable detailed military knowledge and much of the Siegfried Line, Germany's defence against France, was personally designed by him. He has, by constant visits and inspections, encouraged officers and men and assured himself of their general efficiency. The army is loyal to Hitler and admires him.

The German soldier of to-day is taught obedience, but not blind obedience. Discipline is strict, the Germans believing that "spit and polish" is an essential in all military training. A German soldier may look dirty and untidy while on manoeuvres or training, but on guards or after duty and when walking out he turns out clean and smart and takes a real pride in his appearance. No error or misdemeanour is, however, too unimportant to be checked and the Prussian serjeant-major is no legend. It is fundamental that every error, every mistake, however small or even apparently trivial, should be noticed and corrected. On the other hand relations between officers and men are not only good but often cordial. An officer looks upon his men as his children to some extent. This does not prevent him, however, demanding from them the greatest sacrifices if necessary.

Both men and officers were accommodated before the war in excellent barracks, but the standard of food did not compare favourably with that served in the British Army. There was little time for sport, so much had to be learnt in the two years that they were with the army.

Training is Realistic

German military training was and is hard and realistic. Casualties in the last manœuvres before the war were reported to be about four hundred. Great attention has always been paid to fitness (they attributed our success in the last war principally to our physical fitness and love of games), and the hours of work, even before the war, were long and arduous. The army was trained for a Blitzkrieg. Speed was the essential in all military operations. "Push on" at any price; to do nothing is to commit a major military crime, was continually drummed into every officer and man. Supporting weapons co-operated closely with the infantry. The Germans maintain that it is the infantry alone which in the end wins battles. The Panzer divisions and the dive bomber exist only to put the infantry on to the objective. German propaganda never fails to point out that infantry is still "Queen of the Battlefield."

German orders differ considerably from ours. There is no hard and fast sequence for them. Generally speaking, the smaller the operation the more detailed the orders. An operation order for the move of a corps may consist of six to seven lines only.

German "Battle Drill"

The German Army is an exponent of "battle drill." For this reason their methods have often been described as "stereotyped."

This is, however, quite a wrong conception of German tactics. The Germans insist that certain things must be carried out in a certain way, e.g., a frontal attack will, when possible, be combined with a flank attack whether the attack is being carried out by a section or an army. Within this framework, however, the German officer, N.C.O. and man is left great latitude.

A task is set with clearly defined limits, but within these limits the maximum initiative is encouraged and demanded. There is, in fact, no bar on initiative provided the fundamentals of "battle drill" are observed. But the initiative shown must be "trained initiative," based on knowledge and not ignorance. "All formalism in tactics is bad" say German military publications, "Success in battle depends on the determination of the individual" is an axiom.

Assault parties, creeping forward with explosives and perhaps flame throwers, are a normal feature of infantry technique: so normal, indeed, that a humorous article in a German paper gives the following advice to troops on leave (if they ever get it—for German troops in war-time get very little). When they return home from Russia to the unfamiliar surroundings of Germany they must be careful to respect civilian habits almost forgotten at the front. If the front door is shut, the proper thing is not to blow it open with a charge in the usual way; for the custom of the country is to ring the bell.

Far From Home

This story throws light on a grievance which German troops often feel. Their pay is good, their rations much better than those of civilians; but leave is very scarce, and they hate being away from home. They have, besides, home anxieties of a kind foreign to us. The files of a Coast Defence Battery in Norway contain a curious instance of the complexities of German life and administration.

Gunner Palenga's home is in Silesia, near a thousand miles away. There his wife lives with her mother. The mother comes under the displeasure of the

Party, and is given notice to quit her house. He has to get his battery commander to write to the municipal authorities to plead against an order which would turn a serving soldier's wife into the street. Fortunately, he was in time. The officer's application caused the order to be suspended—but only suspended.

Thorough Preparations

The German General Staff, in fact all German officers, are keen students of military history. They examine and re-examine the lessons of past wars in order to deduce from them the main lessons. They believe that preparations are three-quarters of the battle.

German attack tactics are simple and can be explained in a few sentences. The attackers first of all select a point at which they will make their main effort. This they call a "Schwerpunkt," or point of main effort. The German officer is taught "An attack without a Schwerpunkt is like a man without character," but if he has chosen the wrong point for his Schwerpunkt he is prepared to change it immediately.

If the battle is an encounter battle, e.g., an advanced guard action, they are prepared to run great risks, even to the length of dispensing with reconnaissance in order to surprise and overwhelm the enemy before he has time to take counter-measures. They invariably try to combine a frontal attack with an outflanking attack.

Trained for Offensive

On the other hand, for a deliberate attack no preparation can be too careful. Reconnaissance after reconnaissance is carried out in order that all commanders should have the best information about the enemy. Every man, weapon and machine is then thrown into the battle at the spot where they hope to obtain a decisive result. Again they try to combine a frontal with a flank attack.

Infiltration tactics are an essential part of all attacks, whether frontal or flanking.

In defence there is one cardinal principle—depth. "Not lines but localities must be defended. Fire is the principal weapon of the defence." So runs the German doctrine. The German Army, however, is primarily trained for the offensive. It dislikes assuming the defensive because it knows that it can never obtain a decision by that means. The present defensive battles on the Russian front are regarded as a prelude to offensive operations and not of any military value in themselves.

When the German Army took the field in 1939 it was an army with a tradition of defeat behind it. Its successes in this war have, to some extent, eradicated this feeling, but even now, at the back of the minds of all German officers and men is the knowledge that in 1918 the German Army was decisively beaten in the field. Two of its former opponents, the British Empire and the U.S.A., are again ranged against it and the German soldier must feel that these two opponents will in the end get the better of him. His determination will not, however, be easily broken. He is cunning and crafty and an aptitude for soldiering is in his blood. He is also tough, otherwise he would not have stood the strain of this war.

A British soldier with a captured damaged 'Goliath' in Italy. The tiny fully tracked Goliath was technically a *Leichter Ladungsträger* (light load or charge carrier). The idea of remote-controlled vehicles for mine clearance had been pioneered in 1939. The Goliath, produced in various models from 1942 to 1945, could be used in mine fields, or to deliver demolition charges to their target.

A 7.5 cm mountain howitzer firing in support of *Gebirgsjäger* ('mountain troops')
Regiment 100 on the Eastern Front. Small howitzers were attached directly to
mountain infantry regiments with heavier guns deployed in mountain artillery
units. Though relatively short range, mountain guns were lighter and
handier than standard pieces.

Men of 97th Jäger (light infantry) Division with a 7.5cm infantry
gun. The sniper, viewing through his telescopic sight over the gun
shield, has a Russian Mosin Nagant rifle. Captured Soriet PPsh sub-
machine guns also saw significant use on the Eastern Front.

Major Günter Goebel
Träger des Eichenlaubs
zum Ritterkreuz des Eisernen Kreuzes

Aufnahme Binz
Film · Foto · Verlag

R 329

Major Günter Goebel, holder of the Knight's Cross with Oak Leaves, from a German
postcard series. Goebel won both grades of the Iron Cross and the Knight's Cross
on the Eastern Front in 1941 when serving with 79th Infantry Division, and the
Oak Leaves in 1943 leading his own battle group. The Knight's Cross, which
ranked above the Iron Cross, was instituted in 1939, and the Oak Leaves in 1940.

Portrait of an infantryman at Mühlhausen in Thuringia, ca.1943. His *Feldbluse* (field jacket) is adorned with buttonhole ribbons for the Iron Cross, Second Class, and the Eastern Front winter campaign medal of 1941–42. The badges on the pocket are, left, the black badge denoting one or two wounds and, right, the infantry assault badge depicting a wreath and rifle awarded for three attacks, counter attacks or armed reconnaissance actions.

CHAPTER 5
Handbook on German Army Identification 1943

The US *Handbook on German Army Identification,* prepared at the Military Intelligence Training Center in Ritchie, Maryland, and issued in April 1943, was far from exhaustive and, despite its title, only about half its contents were about the German Army. It contained no really new information, nor was it infallible. Indeed its foreword was something of a disclaimer, remarking 'the need for such a manual was so pressing that some errors and omissions are anticipated in the current edition'. Nevertheless this seventy-seven-page booklet remains significant, attractive and even collectible. For what it managed to do, with its lively graphic style and popular upbeat presentation, was to engage the reader in a way achieved by few Second World War manuals. The *Handbook on German Army Identification* was not wordy, dry or difficult to understand but used clever design and simple cartoon-like illustrations to convey messages.

Such use of lively line drawing figures and sketches went back to the First World War when a number of close combat and trench warfare manuals pioneered this style. Privately produced inter-war German manuals continued the approach, as did some US Army field manuals, albeit in a less overtly mannered fashion. Humour and artistry were also embraced by pamphlets of British Home Guard enthusiasts. Yet arguably, the *Handbook on German Army Identification* was a leader in the new wave of genuinely popular training literature inspired by the cartoon and certainly bears comparison with enemy productions such as the *Tigerfibel* ('Tiger tank primer') of August 1943 or the overtly weird anti-tank booklet *Der Panzerknacker* ('the tankbuster') of 1944.

The pages selected here concentrate specifically on the German Army and on those aspects of identification that US servicemen really needed to know. Essentially they tell us what the ordinary German soldier looked like, what he wore and what and where his rank insignia were. Other parts of the booklet gave basic information on specialist badges, the Airforce, Navy, *Schutzstaffel* (*SS*) and other political formations, as well as the meanings of German road signs.

HANDBOOK

ON

German Army Identification

1943

War Department—The Military Intelligence Training Center—Camp Ritchie, Md.

The 'Conscription Duties of the German Citizen', from the US *Handbook on German Army Identification*, 1943. A neat way of explaining to the American serviceman the basic path through German military and paramilitary service. Soldier's personal documents also reflected these stages.

German Rifleman
Deutscher Schütze

Helmet, brim type, belt (Koppel), leather, buckle showing (Koppel-schloss). Ammunition pouches, 3 each side, bayonet, short, sharp spade.

FRONT VIEW

LEFT SIDE

Gas mask over right hip, canteen (Feldflasche) and rations bag (Brotbeutel). Long trousers tucked into half-length boots.

BACK VIEW

RIGHT SIDE

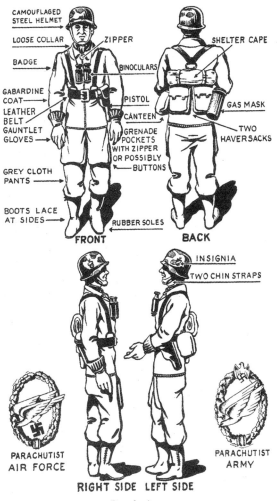

Parachutists

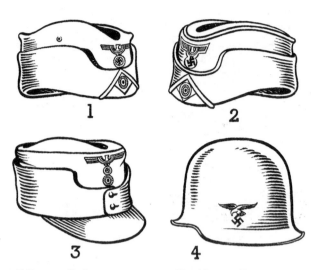

1. Field cap, enlisted men
2. Field cap, officers, turn-up, badge, crown piped with silver
3. Mountain cap, officers and enlisted men
4. Parachutists helmet (air force); can also show Hoheitsabzeichen (infantry)

8 is the personal number. Stb. means Staff. 7 Pz. Abw. means 7th Division Antitank Battalion. Blood group "O"

83 is the personal number. 1st Company of 111th Infantry Regiment (formerly of 87th Infantry Regiment). Blood group "O"

e. National Insignia of the Armed Forces (Hoheitsabzeichen der Wehrmacht).

Mützen-Hoheitsabzeichen Luftwaffe (cap national insignia of air force)

Mützen-Hoheitsabzeichen, Heer silbern, Kriegsmarine golden (cap national insignia, Army silver, Navy gold)

Hoheitsabzeichen für Rock u. Feldbluse (national insignia for coat and field blouse of the air force)

Hoheitsabzeichen für Rock u. Feldbluse, Heer silbern, Kriegsmarine golden (national insignia for coat and field blouse; Army silver, Navy gold)

Left side

Right side

Stahlhelm Luftwaffe (steel helmet, air force)

Left side

Right side

Stahlhelm für Heer und Kriegsmarine (steel helmet for Army and Navy)

a. Company officers.

Leutnant (second lieutenant). Lowest ranking officer. No stars on shoulder straps

Oberleutnant (first lieutenant). Shoulder strap has one gold star

Hauptmann (Rittmeister in the cavalry) (captain). Two gold stars on shoulder straps

b. Field officers.

Major (major). Shoulder strap has no star

Oberstleutnant (lieutenant colonel). One gold star on shoulder strap

Oberst (colonel). Two gold stars on shoulder strap

c. *Band masters.*—Band masters rate a salute from all noncommissioned officers and enlisted men. However, they do not outrank any commissioned officers even though they may hold a higher corresponding rank.

NONCOMMISSIONED OFFICERS

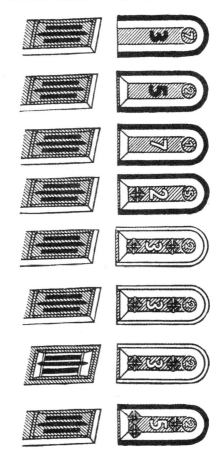

Unteroffizier (sergeant). Only noncommissioned officer with silver strip open on arm end. Embroidered number of regiment or battalion in color of arm of service

Unterfeldwebel (cavalry: unterwachtmeister). Number of regiment or battalion in color of arm of service

Fähnrich (officer aspirant junior grade). Same as Unterfeldwebel, only numbers of regiment or battalion in silver. This grade has lately been abolished

Feldwebel (or Wachtmeister, cavalry) (technical sergeant). Shoulder straps same as above with one dull silver star

Oberfeldwebel or Oberwachtmeister (battalion sergeant major, approximate American equivalent). Same as Feldwebel, but with two silver stars

Hauptfeldwebel or Hauptwachtmeister (first sergeant). Shoulder strap same as Oberfeldwebel. Also has two silver stripes on both lower sleeves

Oberfähnrich (officer aspirant senior grade). Shoulder strap same as Oberfeldwebel, but he has officer's collar patch. This grade has lately been abolished

Stabsfeldwebel or Stabswachtmeister (regimental sergeant major). Same shoulder straps as Feldwebel, but with three silver stars

ENLISTED MEN

Schütze (private). No chevron

Oberschütze (private first class). One dull silver diamond

Gefreiter (lance corporal). One dull silver chevron

Obergefreiter (corporal) with less than 6 years service. Two dull silver chevrons

Obergefreiter (corporal) with more than 6 years service. One dull silver chevron and one diamond

Stabsgefreiter (corporal on administrative duty). Two dull silver chevrons and one diamond

CHAPTER 6
Personal Documents

Wehrpaß and *Soldbuch* (service record and pay book)
The *Wehrpaß* was the permanent record of service and remained with an individual from its issue until the joining of a military unit. Early examples showed the army eagle and swastika on the cover, later types, like that depicted, the 'national' emblem or *Hoheitszeichen*. When the individual was inducted into a unit the *Wehrpaß* was handed in and a *Soldbuch* issued. This allowed the drawing of pay and acted as a personal identity document. When a period of service was completed the *Wehrpaß* was filled in and returned to the individual.

Wehrpaß: **front cover**
The *Wehrpaß* was bound in grey-green leather-grained card. This *Papyrolin* was a stable mixture of paper with textile fibres. The 'H' in the lower box stands

for *Heer* ('army'), the 'E' in the small upper right box is the initial letter of the surname of the holder, Georg Eisele. This particular *Wehrpaß* was printed by Metten and company of Berlin in February 1939.

Wehrpaß: inner cover
Under the front cover was a small pocket for loose items, an index to the booklet, and a warning against misuse. Opposite are the holder's name and the numbers from his *Arbeitsbuch* ('employment booklet') and military identity tag. Eisele's *Wehrpaß* was issued by a staff officer in the Mannheim military headquarters sub-district in July 1940.

Wehrpaß: pages 2–3
Next to the photo and signature of Georg Eisele are his personal details. He was a Protestant German citizen born in Heidelberg on 12 July 1902. He was unmarried, and his parents, Georg senior, a carpenter, and Anna, were still alive at the time of document issue. Georg junior was a metal worker or locksmith.

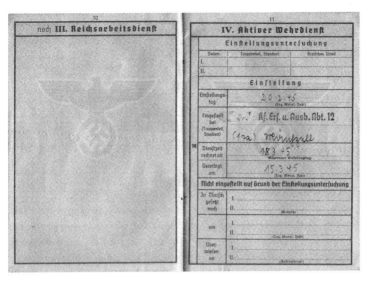

10	
noch III. Reichsarbeitsdienst	

11
IV. Aktiver Wehrdienst

Einstellungsuntersuchung

	Datum	Truppenteil, Standort	Ärztliches Urteil
I.			
II.			

Einstellung

Einstellungs-tag	20.2.45 *(Tag, Monat, Jahr)*
Eingestellt bei (Truppenteil, Standort)	Kf. Erf. u. Ausb. Abt. 12 (17a) Mannheim
Dienstzeit rechnet ab	18.3.45 *(Maßgebender Einstellungstag)*
Deceibigt am	15.3.45 *(Tag, Monat, Jahr)*

Nicht eingestellt auf Grund der Einstellungsuntersuchung

In Marsch gesetzt noch	I.	
	II.	*(Maßstelle)*
am	I.	
	II.	*(Tag, Monat, Jahr)*
Über-wiesen an	I.	
	II.	*(Wehrbezirk)*

Wehrpaß: **pages 10-11**

Pages 8-10 recorded time with the *Reichsarbeitsdienst* ('state labour service'). Labour service was for those aged eighteen to twenty-five, but Eisele was already over thirty when this became compulsory and these pages are blank. He was in his middle forties by the time he was called upon to bear arms – his enlistment being doubtless delayed due to his age, profession and perhaps other circumstances. It was February 1945 before he joined motor transport supply troop replacement and Training Battalion 12 at Mannheim. His duration of service was less than two months; the area was overrun by the US Army in late March 1945.

Soldbuch: **cover**

The *Soldbuch* of Franz Wirtz, issued in June 1940, shows the typical tan leather-grain *Papyrolin* cover and national emblem. Troops were instructed to carry the *Soldbuch* in the uniform jacket pocket for identification; unsurprisingly therefore surviving examples are often in poorer condition than the *Wehrpaß* which typically spent much of its time in office files or the soldier's home.

Soldbuch: **inner cover**

Photos of *Soldbuch* holders were added in 1944 as a security measure. In this case, the picture of Franz Wirtz was probably taken in 1943 as his uniform is that of an *Unteroffizier* (junior NCO). However, this photo is likely to have been attached or re-attached late in 1944 or early in 1945, since the rubber stamps validating the image do not also cover part of the picture as was intended. On

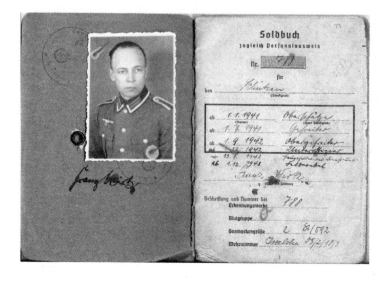

the right is the number of the *Soldbuch*, which in this instance is the same as that of his *Erkennungsmarke* ('identification tag'). The list of promotions shows a brisk rise through the ranks, for although Wirtz started his army career as a humble *Schütze* ('rifleman') in 1940, he was promoted six times to reach the rank of *Feldwebel* ('sergeant major') on 1 December 1943. Wirtz's blood group is given as 'O' and his gas-mask size as 2 or medium. His *Wehrnummer* (armed forces registration number) was given at Iserlohn near Dortmund.

Soldbuch: **pages 2–3**
Page 2 of the *Soldbuch* gives personal details. Wirtz was born in 1905 at Ohe, in the Oberbergischer Kreis, a Protestant giving his civilian calling as 'city minister'. He was described as 162 cm tall, round-faced and with dark blonde hair and blue eyes. The details were attested by the *Oberleutnant* commander of third company *Landesschützen Ersatz Bataillon 6,* a local defence replacement battalion. On page 3 are full details of promotions, usually signed off by the adjutant of *Landesschützen Bataillon 470* with which Wirtz saw field service.

Soldbuch: pages 4–5

Page 4 traces Wirtz's wartime movements from unit to unit, starting at Iserlohn, through *Festungs* ('fortress infantry battalion') 1404, via Lüdenscheid and Osnabrück, to Köslin (now Koszalin) in Prussia and the defence of the Eastern Front. Page 5 details his wife and parents. His wife's name is underlined in red: whether this marking is related to her Jewish maiden name 'Simon' is unknown.

Soldbuch: clothing and equipment

This is one of several inserts in the *Soldbuch* of Franz Wirtz detailing issues of clothing and equipment. We can see that although he received two *Feldblusen* (uniform field jackets) in 1942 and a fatigue uniform, he was not issued with the *Waffenrock* parade jacket. With his uniform were two sets of underwear, shirts, collars, socks, two forage caps and a peaked cap, lace-up boots, steel helmet, greatcoat and other items. Towards the end of the list are added the *Zeltbahn* (multipurpose 'shelter half' or tent piece) and *Fußlappen* (traditional 'footwraps' worn as an alternative to socks). This particular set of clothing was withdrawn, struck out in red and replaced with a fresh issue in July 1944. This included two blankets and a model 1934 *Tornister* (pack) but omitted the peaked cap. Equipment mentioned on other pages and inserts included handkerchiefs, a hand towel, mug, identity tag, field dressings, bayonet frog, belt, cartridge carriers, helmet net, bread bag, water bottle and braces.

He was also issued with a gas mask, which was retested in August 1944. His final clothing issue was on 30 April 1945, just a week before the end of the war when he was given more socks and a second pair of boots. His weapon, recorded on page 9, was initially the Czech Model 1924 rifle and bayonet, with which eleven entire divisions of the German Army were equipped at the outbreak of war. This was replaced with a captured French rifle in 1943 and, finally, in November 1944 with a P38 semi-automatic pistol.

Soldbuch: **hospital record**

Pages 12 and 13 of the *Soldbuch* record stays in hospital. Wirtz was wounded on the Eastern Front and admitted to the care of a motorised hospital unit on 11 February 1945. His injury is recorded as '31b', the code for a shell wound, which must have been serious as he was still under treatment months after the war ended.

In the back of this *Soldbuch*, together with a selection of printed addenda and health notices, are some cuttings and two small maps from 1955, clarifying what happened a decade earlier. Wirtz had been evacuated by ship from the Memel area, but only as far as Pillau (now Baltiysk), where he found himself trapped within the defensive 'fortress' zone of Königsberg. Here he was wounded some time between 8 and 10 February 1945, and later evacuated again west across the Baltic, arriving in Stralsund on 4 April. The issue of boots and socks at the end of that month suggests that he was by then 'walking wounded'. After repeated bombardment and a three-month siege, the city of Königsberg was completely cut off on 7 April 1945. It was surrendered by its commander General Otto Lasch on 9 April to Russian forces, and is now part of Russia and known as Kaliningrad. Wirtz had a lucky escape.

Soldbuch-Ersatz

The *Soldbuch-Ersatz* was a temporary replacement document for troops whose original had been lost or destroyed. This example was issued by the *Reserve-Lazarett* ('reserve military hospital') at Herborn to *Obergefreiter* Erwin Schwary of *1 Füsilier Bataillon Infanterie Regiment Nr 342* in February 1945. Schwary, in civilian life a plasterer from Mittelhofen, had five years' service and was aged 34 when injured by a shell.

Ausgezahlte Gebührnisbeträge			
am	für (Zeit)	Erläuterungen	RM.
	Reserve-Lazarett Herborn	Obergefr.	

Reserve-Lazarett Herborn (Dillkreis)

Soldbuch-Ersatz

Vor- und Zuname: Erwin Schwary
Dienstgrad: O'Gefr.
Truppenteil: 1. Füs. Batl. 342
F.P.-Nr. 27038 D Diensteintritt: 27.2.40
Beruf: Stuckateur
Geb. am 11.4.10 in Mittelhofen
Beschriftung der Erkennungsmarke: J.Ers.Abtlg.
208 Nr. 1448

evang. — kath. — ggl. — led. — verh. — gesch.
Anschrift der nächsten Angehörigen: Ehefrau — Vater —
Mutter:
Vor- und Zuname: Lina Schwary
Ort: Mittelhofen
Straße oder Post: Bennerrod
Abgang am wohin

Ersatztruppenteil: Aufkl.Ers.u.Ausb.Abtlg 6

Inhaber erhält Kriegsbesoldung — Friedensgebührnisse von der H.-Standort-Gebührnisstelle

Wehrmacht money

German forces issued their own notes for use of personnel and persons 'of the same status' in occupied countries. The first series appeared in 1942, but was replaced by a new issue in September 1944. Along with the ten-Reichsmark note, seen here, the 1944 series included bills for one and five Reichsmarks.

CHAPTER 7
Enemy Weapons 1943

Enemy weapons were of perennial interest to the Allied soldier. As the US *Intelligence Bulletin* of March 1946 observed in light of recent experience:

> Today, most soldiers know that a knowledge of foreign weapons and ma-
> tériel gives a man an insight to the capabilities and limitations of either a
> potential enemy or ally. Many have learned to appreciate the difference
> in bursting radius of a Jap grenade and its Australian counterpart, or the
> difference in range and accuracy between a "burp" gun and a Bren. Yet
> there is another reason why well-trained soldiers should be familiar with
> the operational use of foreign matériel.
>
> Modern warfare is characterized by rapid maneuver dependent
> upon great masses of complex supplies. In the past there have been
> times when a unit, moving too fast for its supply train to keep pace, has
> found itself in great need of such things as ammunition, spare parts for
> motor vehicles, and replacement gun tubes. Very often this need for re-
> plenished supplies has been felt at the crucial and deciding phase of the
> operation. At such times, some commanders and their troops have saved
> their situation, or at least improved their position, by the resourceful use
> of captured foreign matériel.

Manuals featuring foreign weapons predated the First World War, and there were many, both official and privately produced, during the Second World War. In Britain, Barlow and Johnson's pocket-sized *Small Arms Manual* was both widespread in distribution and catholic in coverage, featuring not just British and German small arms but a smattering of US, Austrian and Italian types. Two editions and three reprints appeared in just over 18 months starting in January 1942. Lt Colonel Barlow of the West Yorkshires was well placed to know his subject, having served as a technical officer at the machine-gun school and held positions in weapons design.

In the popular, probably officially inspired volume *The German Army of Today* by Wilhelm Necker (1943) were found not only weapons and organisations but photographs taken direct from German publications. As one reviewer observed: 'Mr Necker has done his best to make his picture as accurate as possible', but soldiers were advised to keep up to date using official 'intelligence summaries'. The official booklet *Enemy Ammunition* ultimately became a whole series of pamphlets encompassing everything from mines, grenades and small arms cartridges to shells and mortar rounds. Colour-illustrated pamphlet 15 of the run appeared a couple of weeks after the end of the war in Europe.

On the other side of the Atlantic, the soldier's bible was US Military Intelligence Special Series issue 14 of May 1943, *German Infantry Weapons*, a systematic coverage ranging from pistols and grenades to the 15 cm heavy infantry howitzer. The stated objective here was to allow American troops to identify and use German arms, the publication being based as far as possible on 'actual examination and operation of the weapons concerned'. This practical experience was supported by 'reports from observers, enemy documents, British publications, and other sources of information'. A particularly useful feature of *German Infantry Weapons* was the inclusion of notes on ammunition and its colour-coded packaging, allowing the GI to work out what suited which

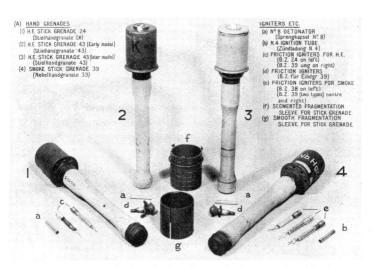

(A) HAND GRENADES
  (1) H.E. STICK GRENADE 24
     (Stielhandgranate '24)
  (2) H.E. STICK GRENADE 43 (Early model)
     (Stielhandgranate '43)
  (3) H.E. STICK GRENADE 43 (later model)
     (Stielhandgranate 43)
  (4) SMOKE STICK GRENADE 39
     (Nebelhandgranate 39)

IGNITERS ETC.
  (a) N° 8 DETONATOR
     (Sprengkapsel N° 8)
  (b) N.4 IGNITION TUBE
     (Zündladung N. 4)
  (c) FRICTION IGNITERS FOR H.E.
     (B.Z. Z4 on left)
     (B.Z. 39 umg on right)
  (d) FRICTION IGNITERS
     (B.Z. für Eindgr 39)
  (c) FRICTION IGNITERS FOR SMOKE
     (B.Z. 38 on left)
     (B.Z. 39 (two types) centre
     and right)
  (f) SEGMENTED FRAGMENTATION
     SLEEVE FOR STICK GRENADE
  (g) SMOOTH FRAGMENTATION
     SLEEVE FOR STICK GRENADE

German stick grenades from the files of MI10, April 1945. Left to right: the 1924 model; two versions of the 1943 model and the 1939 smoke grenade. Fragmentation sleeves, igniters and detonators surround the grenades.

weapon and whether rounds were, for example, armour-piercing, practice, dummy or for use in machine guns.

The Germans had made use of instructional films before the end of the First World War, supplementing practical lessons and printed manuals on weapons. The new media scored in terms of interest and engagement and in showing mechanisms and operations obviated the need for complex and wordy descriptions. Not long afterwards both the US and the UK followed suit and during the Second World War the Western Allies also made films showing enemy weapons.

Perhaps the most obvious example of these was US *War Department Film Bulletin*, issue 115 of 1944, *Enemy Weapons – German Infantry Small Arms*, produced by the Signal Corps Photographic Center. Wisely this movie was just twelve minutes long, and selected only the German rifle, the MP 40 sub-machine gun, the MG 34 and MG 42. These were the most likely weapons the Allied infantryman would encounter, and brevity was well calculated to maintain interest. Clearly the ideal was that as many servicemen as possible should be exposed to practical training and training films on enemy arms, and more extensive and comprehensive printed manuals should be available as well. This was important not only because certain troops such as armourers and technicians would require greater technical knowledge, but because films were not always available, nor readily referenced in the field.

The British *Enemy Weapons* series commenced in 1941 with Part I, *German Infantry Weapons*. Part II, issued the following year, covered mainly Italian weapons but also mentioned Austrian arms still in use and gave 'revised particulars' of German weapons, namely the P38 pistol, now recognised as a 'standard' weapon, and the 5 cm mortar. Part III of December 1942 extended the coverage of German material to light anti-aircraft and anti-tank guns. In 1943 Part IV revisited German infantry weapons, but widened the scope still further to heavy artillery. Distribution of the *Enemy Weapons* series was widespread, with print runs of the order of 50,000 copies.

Our subject here is *Enemy Weapons*, Part V, *German Infantry*, *Engineer and Airborne Weapons*, which was issued in July 1943. Most of the manual is reproduced, except the final part which addressed the recoilless airborne gun, the illustrations to which defy quality reproduction. It should also be noted that Part V does not repeat all the information published hitherto but rather fills gaps and adds weapons encountered and recorded recently. So it is that we see one of the earliest weapons, the MP 18 sub-machine gun, cheek by jowl with the G41 semi-automatic rifle and the still new MG 42 machine gun. Attempts have been made to compensate for this partial coverage by the inclusion of illustrations of other German weapons elsewhere in this book.

The *Karabiner 98 kurz* (*K98k*) rifle fitted with a sniper scope, teamed with observers with periscopes and binoculars, from a German infantry weapons postcard series.

A *Gefreiter* (lance corporal) of the mountain troops with a captured Russian Maxim machine gun quadruple anti-aircraft mounting. Multiple barrels put more rounds in the air quickly in an attempt to compensate for the increasing speed of aircraft.

An example of a 1941 label for rifle grenade detonator packaging complete with application instructions from a secret draft of a file that later fell into British intelligence hands.

26/GS Publications/983

THIS DOCUMENT MUST NOT FALL INTO ENEMY HANDS

ENEMY WEAPONS

PART V—GERMAN INFANTRY, ENGINEER, AND AIRBORNE WEAPONS

1943
Crown Copyright Reserved
Prepared under the direction of The Chief of the Imperial General Staff
THE WAR OFFICE,
July, 1943.

ENEMY WEAPONS

PART V—GERMAN INFANTRY, ENGINEER AND AIRBORNE WEAPONS

SECTION I—GERMAN GRENADES AND GRENADE DISCHARGERS

1. Introductory note
In addition to the familiar egg and stick hand grenades (described in Enemy Weapons Part I) several new types of grenade, both HE and AP, have been developed recently. These are fired from two different rifle attachments, and from a modified signal pistol.

2. 27 mm Grenade pistol (Kampfpistole) (Fig 1)
This is a modification of a standard German signal pistol. The pistol is constructed of a light metal alloy, has a rifled barrel, and carries a small dial sight on the left side. The grenade is in the form of a small nose-fuzed HE round

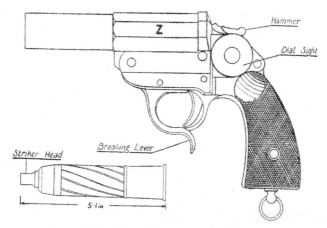

Fig 1—27 mm GRENADE AND SIGNAL PISTOL

and is fired up to a maximum range of approximately 100 yards. The pistol will not fire British Verey pistol ammunition. Smoke and indicating rounds (orange smoke) are also in service. The bases of the HE, smoke, and indicating cartridges are marked SPR. Z, NEBEL. Z and DEUT. Z, respectively.

(*a*) *General particulars*

Calibre	27 mm (1 in)
Weight of pistol	1 lb 9½ oz
Length of pistol	9¾ in
Weight of complete round	5 oz
Length of complete round	5·1 in
Length of projectile with fuze	4·4 in
Type of filling	Penthrite wax

(*b*) *Preparation for firing*

Break the pistol by pressing down lever forming part of trigger guard. Load grenade and close pistol smartly.

3. Rifle discharger (cup type) (Schiessbecher) (Fig 2—6)

(*a*) *The discharger* (Fig 2).—This is made of steel, and consists of a rifled barrel which screws into a holder fitted with a clamp for attaching to the rifle

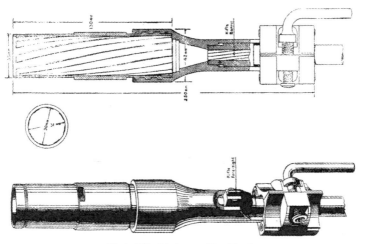

Fig 2—Rifle Discharger (Cup Type)

barrel. There are no gas ports, and varying ranges are obtained by altering the elevation of the rifle with the aid of a sighting attachment. With practice, however, the discharger can be used effectively without the sight.

(b) *Ammunition* (Figs 3–5)

    (i)   Three types of grenade are fired, two of which are armour piercing in different sizes and the third anti-personnel with provision for throwing as a hand grenade.

    (ii) *Small AP grenade (Gewehr Panzergranate)* (Fig 3)

This grenade incorporates the hollow charge principle, *i.e.*, a shaped cavity is formed at the forward end of the HE filling with the result that, on impact, a jet of blast is concentrated in a forward direction. It follows, therefore, that the penetration of armour is equal at all ranges, since it depends on this jet and not on the striking velocity of the projectile. The difficulty of hitting the target, however, restricts the use of this grenade to ranges up to 100 yards. It is only likely to be effective against lightly armoured targets.

The body is made in two parts: a forward portion of steel containing the bursting charge and hollow charge cone, closed by a light metal cap, and a rear portion of light aluminium alloy containing the fuze and exploder system. A pre-engraved driving band is formed at 6 mm from the rear end of the grenade.

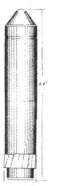  

Fig 3—Small AP Grenade   Fig 4—Large AP Grenade

Fig 5—Anti-Personnel Grenade

Other details are as follows:—

Total weight	8·8 oz
Overall length	6·4 in
Weight of filling	1·75 oz

(iii) *Large AP grenade* (*Gross Gewehr Panzergranate*) (Fig 4)

This grenade is constructed on similar general lines to (ii) above, except that the front portion is enlarged and contains a greater bursting charge. The total weight of the grenade is approximately 12¾ oz, the weight of the bursting charge 4¼ oz. This grenade and the one described at (ii) above should be handled with great care, as they arm very easily.

The other end, facing the firer when the sight is assembled to the rifle, is inscribed with a range scale graduated from 25–100 metres in steps of 25 metres. To give the desired range, the body is rotated and the appropriate graduation brought opposite a pointer on the carrier plate. The body is then held in position by a ball and spring detent.

(c) *Ammunition* (Fig 8)

    (i)   Only one type of ammunition has been identified to date. This is a hollow charge anti-tank grenade with a tubular tail which fits over the spigot of the discharger. The grenade is grey-green in colour.

    (ii) The head is bell shaped and contains the explosive filling, which is hollowed out to a depth of ·79 in and contained by a concave aluminium diaphragm. The head is closed by a slightly convex metal cap.

(iii) The fuze body, which is cylindrical, screws into the base of the head. Pressure on firing acts on a cutting pin, the base of which is flush with the base of the fuze. This shears a safety pin which is ejected by a spring. The firing pin can then set forward on impact into the detonator.

(iv) The tail screws into the base of the fuze. It is tubular and has six tail fins near the base.

(v) The grenade is propelled by means of a wooden bulleted blank cartridge. Until needed, this is carried in the tail tube of the grenade which is closed by a rubber plug.

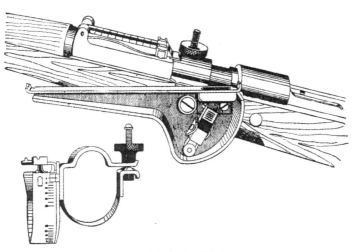

Fig 6—Sight for Cup Discharger

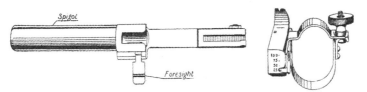

Fig 7—Rifle Discharger (Spigot Type) and Sight

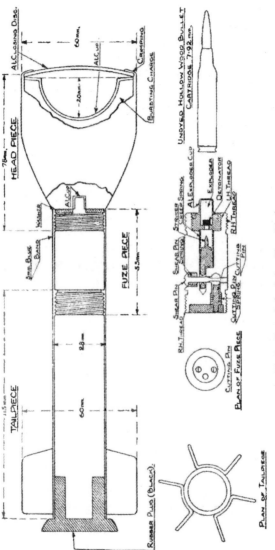

Fig 8—Grenade for Spigot Type Discharger

Section 2—GERMAN MACHINE CARBINES

5. Introductory note

In addition to the machine carbines described in *Enemy Weapons, Part I*, it has been established that the weapons described below are standard in the German Army. The 9 mm machine carbines, MP38 and MP40, described in *Enemy Weapons, Part I*, Sec **4**, are still, however, the most widely used.

It should be noted that although many of these weapons are sighted up to 1,000 metres, they will rarely be used at ranges above 200 yards.

6. 9 mm machine carbine MP18[1] (Bergmann) (Fig 9)

(*a*) The MP18[1], first introduced towards the end of the last war, is the original German machine carbine.

It is operated in common with all later types by blowback and carries on the left a 32-round drum magazine of rather complicated design consisting of a short straight portion terminating in a small drum.

(*b*) *General particulars*

Calibre	9 mm (·35 in)
Weight (without magazine)	9 lb 2½ oz
Length	32 in

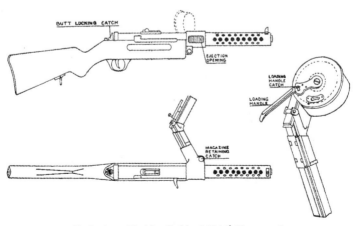

Fig 9—9 mm Machine Carbine MP 18[1] (Bergmann)

Cyclic rate of fire	550 rpm
Ammunition	9 mm parabellum
Sights	Barleycorn foresight and "V" backsight graduated for 100 and 200 metres

(c) *Safety*

A safety recess marked "S" is formed at the rear end of the cocking handle slot.

(d) *To load magazine*

Turn the lever on the bottom of the magazine until a catch drops into a recess in the bottom plate, thereby taking off the tension of the coil spring. Insert the cartridges into the mouth of the magazine. After fully charging the magazine, release the catch and pressure will be applied to the cartridges by the spring.

(e) *Preparation for firing*

Pull back cocking handle and rotate upwards into safety recess. Insert full magazine in feedway. Disengage cocking handle from safety recess. The weapon is now ready for firing. There is no provision for firing single shots.

(f) *Stripping*

Remove magazine and see that machine carbine is cleared and uncocked.

Press in the butt locking catch. Tip the barrel downwards so that the body is clear of the butt. Rotate body end cap to the left and remove with return spring. Remove bolt and striker; using the return spring rod, press out extractor.

7. 9 mm machine carbine MP28[11] (Schmeisser) (Not illustrated)

(a) The MP28[11] is another pre-war blowback operated weapon, many mechanical features of which are incorporated in the MPs 38 and 40. With its wooden stock and perforated barrel casing, it is not unlike the MP18[1] in appearance, but carries a straight 32 round box magazine on the left. Provision is made for firing single shots.

(b) *General particulars*

Calibre	9 mm (·35 in)
Weight	9 lb
Length	31½ in
Cyclic rate of fire	550 rpm
Ammunition	9 mm parabellum
Sights	Barleycorn foresight and "V" backsight graduated up to 1000 metres

(c) *Preparation for firing*

The change lever is in the form of a bar fitted in the trigger guard. For single shot fire, press bar over to right side so that letter "E" is exposed, for automatic fire press bar to left side exposing letter "D".

In other respects for safety, preparation for firing, and stripping, proceed as for the MP18[1].

8. 9 mm machine carbine MP34[1] (Bergmann) (Fig 10)

(*a*) This weapon, although not listed as a standard machine carbine, is known to be in service to some extent. Of more complicated design than the MP18[1] it incorporates two safety devices, a catch operating on the trigger and a cocking piece preventing movement of the cocking handle. Provision is made for single shot and automatic fire.

(*b*) *General particulars*

Calibre	9 mm (·35 in)
Weight	9 lb
Length	32¾in
Cyclic rate of fire	850 rpm
Ammunition	9 mm parabellum
Sights	Barleycorn foresight and "V" backsight graduated to 1,000 metres

(*c*) *Preparation for firing*

Pull back safety catch (on left of body, below back sight) to "F" (fire). Rotate cocking handle anti-clockwise through 90° and pull back. Push forward again and return to original position. Set safety catch to "S" (safe), and insert a filled magazine in feedway.

(*d*) *Stripping*

Remove magazine and ensure that chamber is empty. Set safety catch to "F". Rotate cocking handle anti-clockwise through 90° and pull back. Depress bolt retaining plunger situated to rear of safety catch and withdraw cocking piece and breech block.

To remove cocking piece from breech block, press cocking piece forward and rotate clockwise through 90°. Withdraw cocking piece, return spring and firing pin from breech block.

To assemble proceed in reverse order. When assembled, the arrow on the cocking piece must coincide with the arrow on the breech block.

(*e*) *Firing*

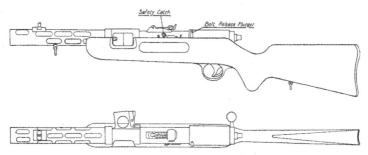

Fig 10—9 mm Machine Carbine MP 34[1] (Bergmann)

There are two triggers, the front one being slotted at the base to allow it to lie pressed independently of the second trigger.

For single shot, the front trigger only is used and is pressed in the normal manner.

For automatic fire, press backwards and downwards on the base of the front trigger. This action depresses both triggers and automatic fire will continue as long as this pressure is maintained or rounds are available in the magazine.

9. 9 mm machine carbine MP34([1])—Steyr-Solothurn

This weapon was described and illustrated in *Enemy Weapons, Part I*, Sec 5. The German name MP34([1]) indicates that the carbine was originally in Austrian service, but has now been adopted for issue to the German Army.

In contrast to the majority of machine carbines it does not fire the standard 9 mm parabellum, but is chambered for the long 9 mm Mauser cartridge which is not interchangeable with British ammunition.

In some models provision is made for attaching a bayonet.

Section 3—GERMAN RIFLES

10. General

(*a*) Rifles and carbines were described in *Enemy Weapons Part I*, Sec **11.** It should be noted that short barrelled rifles, of various marks, though differing only very slightly in design, are now the most frequently encountered in regular units. The later models are usually fitted with tunnel foresight protectors and moulded plastic muzzle caps in place of the original combined protector and muzzle cap of metal.

(*b*) In the following section, a new self-loading rifle is described. It should not be assumed however that this weapon is intended to replace the bolt-operated rifle. This still remains the principal personal weapon of the infantry, supported by a proportion of machine carbines and self-loading rifles.

11. Rifles

(*a*) *7·92 mm self-loading rifle (Gewehr* 41(W)) (Fig 11)

This rifle is a comparatively recent addition to German infantry armament. It is self-loading, *i.e.,* on pressing the trigger, one round is fired and the surplus gas pressure operates the self-loading mechanism to eject the spent case, and reload and cock the rifle. The energy is supplied by the pressure of gas trapped in a cylinder at the muzzle of the rifle, which pressure drives a floating piston and connecting rod to the rear.

(*b*) *General particulars*

Calibre	7·92 mm (·31 in)
Weight	10 lb 14 oz
Overall length	45 in
Feed	rectangular box magazine incorporated in trigger guard.
Magazine capacity	10 rounds
Sights	leaf backsight graduated from 100–1,200 metres
Ammunition	standard 7·92 mm SAA

(*c*) *Safety*

Safety catch at rear end of body, rotated to the right for "safe" and to the left for "fire."

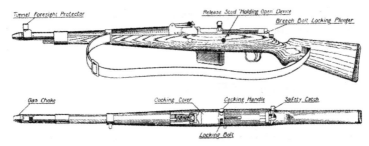

Fig 11—7·92 mm Self-Loading Rifle (Gewehr 41 (W))

(*d*) *Locking bolt*

When the breech bolt is withdrawn to the rear, a locking bolt can be applied. This operates through the cocking cover and holds the main spring compressed and facilitates removal and assembly of breech bolt to body.

(*e*) *Preparation for firing*

Withdraw breech bolt to rear of body. Place a charger vertically in guides. Force cartridges down until top cartridge is clear of charger and held in magazine. Repeat with second charger to fill magazine. Allow breech bolt to go forward and feed top cartridge into chamber by depressing plunger on left of body.

(*f*) *Strip for cleaning*

Withdraw breech bolt to rear of body and apply locking bolt by pressing over to right. Rotate safety catch to the right—"safe."

Push in the locking plunger at rear end of breech bolt, raise rear end of breech bolt, and withdraw from body. Rotate safety catch to left, press trigger to release tension on hammer. Cleaning rod or pull-through can now be used.

(*g*) *Normal cleaning after firing*

Withdraw breech bolt to rear of body and apply locking bolt. Pull-through can now be used.

(*h*) *To assemble breech bolt to rifle*

Rotate safety catch to left, "Fire". Depress hammer until it engages with sear bent. Rotate safety catch to right, "Safe". Insert breech bolt in body, keeping the front end down, and move slightly forward.

Depress plunger at rear end to allow rear end of breech bolt cover to take up its position in body.

Release pressure on locking plunger and rotate safety catch to the left.

Note.—Particular care should be taken to ensure that the breech bolt is oiled, only the bolt face being left dry.

Section 4—GERMAN MACHINE GUNS

12. Introductory note

Three new German MGs have been brought into use since 1941. One of these, the MG 42, described below in Sec **13,** has already been introduced into several German units, where it has replaced the MG 34. It is not expected, however, that a complete change over will take place in the near future, so that the MG 34 is likely to be met in the field for some time to come. The other two MGs, briefly described in Secs **14** and **15,** are regarded as experimental models, but are included here as they are known to have been in service to some extent.

13. 7·92 mm dual purpose MG—MG 42 (Figs 12-13)

(*a*)   This is the new standard dual purpose MG in the German Army, and is in process of replacing the MG 34.

The gun has a high cyclic rate of fire (about 1,200 rpm) obtained by the improved design of breech and feed mechanism, and is provided with a rapid and efficient barrel changing device. The extensive use of pressings in place of machined parts in the construction is a notable feature from the production point of view. German documents give the cyclic rate of fire as 1,500 rpm.

On the other hand, accuracy is not as high as with the MG 34, and there is no provision for single shot fire.

(*b*)   *General particulars*

Weight with bipod	23¾ lb
Overall length	48 in
Cyclic rate of fire	1,100–1,150 rpm
System of operation	Short recoil to unlock action, then blow back.
Feed	Flexible metal belt containing 50 rounds (two or more of these may be joined end to end). A drum holding one 50 round belt may be fitted on left of gun.
Weight of tripod	43 lb 5 oz.

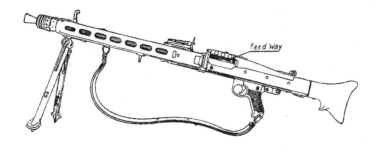

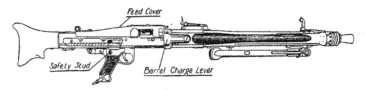

Fig 12—7·92 mm Dual Purpose MG—MG 42

(c) *Safety*

A press stud is provided on the pistol grip. With the letter "S" exposed, the action is safe. With the letter "F" exposed, the action is ready for firing.

(d) *Preparation for firing as LMG*

Prepare bipod for firing; to adjust height, rotate screw between bipod legs until the desired height is obtained. Raise foresight pillar and adjust back sight to the required setting.

Pull back the cocking handle and return to forward position. If the belt is provided with a loading tag, insert this tag in the feed opening and draw through the feed block, with the feed cover closed, as far as it will go, when the first round in the belt will be opposite the chamber. In the absence of the tag, empty the first two links of the belt, raise the feed cover, and place the belt in the feed block with the first round central.

(e) *Removal of belt*

Cock the action, set safety catch to "safe". Raise the feed cover and lift out the belt.

Set safety catch to "fire". Press trigger and allow the recoiling portion to move forward under control. Close the body cover.

(f)   *Partial stripping*

After a period of continuous fire when the barrel has become hot, it should be changed as follows:—

    (i)   Cock the action and set to safe.

    (ii)   Press forward barrel change lever catch, and swing out lever to the right. Remove barrel, using asbestos gloves, tongs, or by tilting the muzzle.

    (iii)   Place new barrel in body, ensuring flanges on muzzle have entered the piston correctly. Close barrel change lever, and ensure that the catch has engaged.

(g)   *Stripping*

    (i)   *Barrel.*—Cock the action, push in barrel change lever catch, move barrel change lever outwards, and remove barrel.

    (ii)   *Butt.*—To remove butt, depress stud on underside, rotate butt and pull to the rear.

    (iii)   *Buffer housing.*—Depress catch on underneath. Rotate quarter turn to right, and pull back.

    To return: Replace buffer into body with cut-away portions on forward lug of buffer housing downwards, rotate quarter turn to left, and ensure catch has engaged.

    (iv)   *Bolt.*—Withdraw bolt to rear, and remove from body. To strip bolt, hold bolt head, rotate bolt tail quarter turn and separate, remove "push piece" from tail. Remove ejector, locking wedge and firing pin from bolt head, remove extractor.

    (v)   *Feed cover and feed block.*—Lift cover and feed block to a vertical position, rotate hinge pin until its cut-away portion is clear of the flange on the body, then withdraw hinge pin to the left.

    Remove feed cover and feed block.

    (vi)   *Feed mechanism.*—Press in spring catch at front end, lift out feed arm. Press bullet guide cover to the rear and allow to spring up on its hinge.

    Lift out connecting link and feed pawls.

    (vii)   *Pistol grip.*—Remove split pin and bush at rear end of pistol grip. Move grip to the rear, and lift away from body.

    (viii)   *Ejection opening cover.*—After removal of pistol grip, the ejection opening cover can be removed by sliding rear end of hinge pin towards centre of body, and removing.

To replace: reverse above operation. Care must be taken to ensure that the spiral spring is in correctly, so as to retain the cover in the open position.

(ix) *Cocking handle.*—Pull cocking handle to the rear, depress lever on skirt of handle, and remove assembly from gun.

(x) *Bipod.*—To remove from body: force bipod assembly to the rear until the spring plunger in the rear of the hinge assembly is depressed, and pull away from body.

To assemble: replace plunger in body, force down, and replace forward end of hinge in body.

(xi) *Muzzle attachment.*—Raise catch and unscrew muzzle attachment. Remove cylinder from outer casing of muzzle attachment.

To assemble: reverse the above procedure.

To remove piston: raise muzzle attachment catch, move piston to rear, rotate until clear of any obstructions, withdraw to rear and remove.

To assemble: reverse the above operations. Care must be taken to ensure that the piston is in correctly so that the cut-away portion of the piston skirt is to the right, and that the piston can be moved completely forward. If this is in incorrectly, the forward travel of the piston is limited.

(xii) *Trigger mechanism.*—Unscrew bolts (two) through side grips, and remove grips.

Remove lower of the two larger axis pins.

Remove top large axis pin.

Remove remaining two small axis pins.

Remove main spring.

Remove sear by rotating half turn to left and withdrawing.

Remove trigger and tripping lever.

Remove change lever by pushing to left, rotating until lug is in line with cut-away slot in left side of grip and removing change lever from pistol grip.

To assemble:

Replace change lever.

Replace tail of sear in tripping lever—replace as one assembly.

Trigger—tripping lever—sear. Replace trigger axis pin (small diameter pin).

Replace main spring axis pin (large pin).

Replace sear axis pin (large pin).

Replace sear lifting pin (small pin).

Replace grips.

Replace grip bolts and nuts.

(xiii) *Assembly.*—Unless otherwise stated, proceed in reverse order.

(*h*) *Immediate action on stoppage*

Remove belt as described. Investigate and remedy stoppage.

Note.—When investigating a feed stoppage by raising the feed cover, the gun should be re-cocked or the cocking handle should be held.

(*i*) *Cleaning and oiling, etc.*

The mechanism should be kept scrupulously clean and well oiled.

The ejection opening cover, which is opened automatically, should be kept closed whenever possible. Precautions should be taken to keep the belts and ammunition clean at all times.

(*j*) *Use as a MMG*

For use as a MMG the gun is mounted on a tripod mounting (Lafette 42). This mounting has a bracket for a dial sight. The trigger of the gun is actuated by means of a trigger lever beside the handle on the right side of the elevating gear.

An automatic searching fire device, operated by the recoil of the gun in the cradle is incorporated. This device elevates the gun step by step and depresses it similarly through a predetermined angle while the gun is firing.

The tripod is very similar to that issued for the MG 34. Points of difference are:

The cradle is not hinged to allow the barrel to be changed (this is of course not necessary for the MG 42).

To disengage the elevating handwheel from the teeth of the stop, the handwheel is pulled out a short distance, instead of a catch being pressed in as with the MG 34 tripod.

Method of attachment of the gun to the tripod is slightly different to suit the different fittings on the gun. The MG 42 cannot be fired from the MG 34 tripod.

14. 7·92 mm MG 34 S

Of the three new guns, this one resembles the MG 34 most closely. Rate of fire is the same, and minor differences in construction do not affect the users' instructions as issued for the MG 34.

15. 7·92 mm MG 34/41

This gun shows an improvement on both MG 34 and 34 S. A higher rate of fire is obtained by an improved breech mechanism which, however, is still basically the same as that of the MG 34. The gun is well constructed and steady to fire from the bipod, but it is thought possible that production considerations have prevented its adoption.

Section 5—GERMAN MORTARS

16. 8 cm (3 in) German mortar 34 (s. Gr. W. 34) (Fig 14)

(This mortar was described in *Enemy Weapons, Part I*, Sec. **16.** A fuller and more up-to-date report is given below.)

(*a*) This is the German equivalent of the British 3-in mortar, and is constructed on similar general lines, *i.e.,* it is a muzzle loading percussion fired weapon, consisting of barrel, bipod, and baseplate. The German mortar has a small shock absorber introduced between the cradle and the bipod, but the chief difference from the British mortar from the user's point of view lies in the cross levelling gear.

In the German gear, rotation of the cross levelling handwheel causes pivotal movement of the elevating screw tube towards or away from the left leg of the bipod and thus alters the transverse level of the traversing gear. A control bolt provided in the breech piece enables the striker to be retracted before unloading should there be a misfire.

(*b*) *General particulars*

Calibre	81·4 mm (3·2 in)
Total weight	125 lb
Elevation	40–90 degrees
Traverse	5½ degrees
Maximum range	2625 yards
No. of charges	5

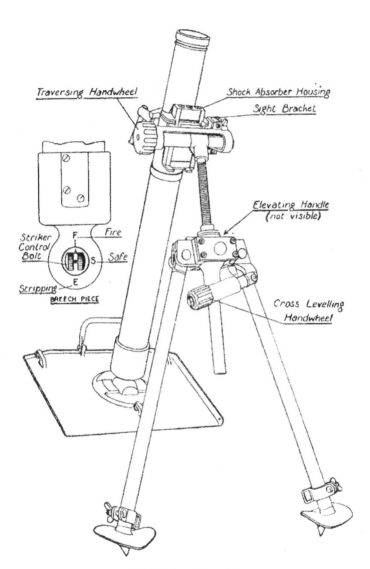

Fig 14—8 cm Mortar 34

| Weight of bomb | 7¾ lb. |
| Rate of fire | 6 rounds in 8–9 secs |

(c) *To set up mortar*

Position base plate. Insert ball on breech cap of barrel in socket of base plate, keeping flat part of ball to the side. Rotate barrel 90 degrees so that sight line painted along barrel is towards firer. Position bipod with elevating handle towards barrel. Open barrel clamping band. Turn elevating handle until about one-third of elevating screw is exposed. Secure clamping band round barrel between clamp position marks. Place sight on barrel and clamp up.

(d) *To load and fire*

Same procedure as for British 3 in mortar.

(e) *Dial sight* (*RA* 35)

The German dial sight differs from the British sight in that both deflection and elevation are graduated in mils instead of degrees and yards. In correcting for line during shooting, if required correction is to the *left* (last round having fallen to the right of the target), the extra deflection must be *added* to the angle on the deflection scales, and if to the right, the extra deflection must be subtracted.

(f) *German procedure in event of misfire*

Wait one minute, and then proceed as follows:—

Make safe by pressing in control bolt and turning it 90 degrees to the right until arrow on head of bolt points to the letter "S" (safe), painted on the breech piece. This action effects withdrawal of the striker.

Loosen the barrel clamping band, rotate the barrel 90 degrees and clamp up again.

Raise the breech end of the barrel until the bomb slides out into the hands of a member of the detachment.

(g) *To change striker*

Lay barrel horizontal. Remove spring ring securing striker in ball of breech cap. With a screwdriver, or the tool provided in the German kit, unscrew striker retaining cap. Press in and rotate control bolt so that arrow points to letter "E". Remove control bolt and spring. Remove striker, using any convenient tool. For insertion of a new striker proceed in reverse order.

(h) *Ammunition* (Fig 15)

Five types of bomb have been identified. These are all nose fuzed streamlined bombs of similar design weighing approximately 7¾. The primary cartridge is fitted centrally in the tail tube and is used alone as Charge I or with one or more secondaries to make up charges 2, 3, 4 or 5.

Details are as follows:—

Type	German name	Markings	Remarks
HE	8 cm Wurfgranate 34	Painted chocolate brown with lettering in black paint.	The standard HE bomb.
HE	8 cm Wurfgranate 38	Painted green. "38" stencilled on body.	Fitted with a rebound charge in the head and bursts 3–20 ft in the air.
HE	8 cm Wurfgranate 39	Painted field grey.	As Wgr 38 but with strengthened head.
Smoke	8 cm Wurfgranate 34 Nb.	Painted dull red. "Nb" stencilled in white on body.	The standard smoke bomb.
Indicator	8 cm Wgr 38 Deut	"Deut" stencilled on body	Used for indicating targets by coloured smoke.

Interchangeability of ammunition

See table at Appendix A.

17. 10 cm (4 in) smoke mortar 35 (10 cm Nebelwerfer 35) (Fig 16)

(*a*) This mortar is a standard smoke weapon in the German Army. HE ammunition, however, is also fired, and the mortar is also nsed to some extent by airborne troops.

(*b*) *The equipment*
This consists of a barrel, base plate, and bipod designed on similar general lines to the 8 cm mortar described in sec **16.** It is, of course, larger and heavier, and the traversing gear is of slightly different design.

(*c*) *Loading and firing*
Proceed as for the 8 cm mortar (sec **16**).

(*d*) *Ammunition*

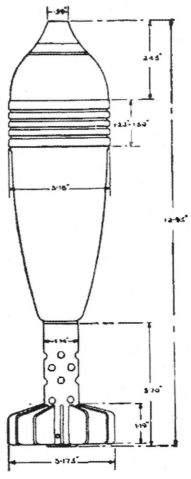

Fig 15—8 cm Mortar Bomb 34

Two types of smoke bomb and a HE bomb are fired. The bombs are similar in design to those fired from the 8 cm mortar.

(e) *General particulars*

Weight in action	231 lb
Weight of barrel	72 lb

Weight of bipod	73 lb
Weight of base plate	83 lb
Weight of bomb	16 lb
Maximum range	3,300 yds
Rate of fire	12–15 rpm
Detachment	5 men

18. 20 cm (7.87 in) spigot mortar (leichte Ladungswerfer) (Figs. 17–18)

(*a*) *General*

This weapon has recently been developed for service in engineer units of the German Army. The mortar throws a heavy HE bomb with a very large charge/weight ratio for comparatively short ranges. The principal task is the destruction of wire, minefields, concrete fieldworks, etc. A smoke bomb is also fired.

(*b*) *General particulars*

Total weight in action	205 lb
Weight of bipod	43 lb
Weight of spigot and supporting arm	73½ lb

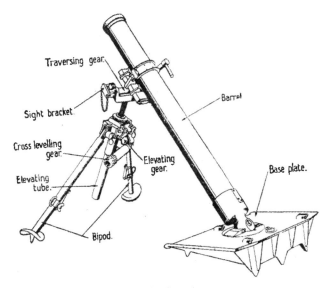

Fig 16—10 cm (4 in) Smoke Mortar 35

Weight of base plate	84 lb
Length of spigot	21·15 in
Diameter of spigot	3·5 in
System of operation	Bomb electrically fired from spigot
Range	766 yards max with 46 lb HE bomb
Sight	Dial sight (Richtaufsatz 39)
Transport	Hand cart

(c) *The equipment*

This consists of a base plate, bipod mounting and spigot with supporting arm.

(i) *The base plate* is of the familiar German mortar design, the bottom being formed with strengthening webs and spikes.

(ii) *The bipod mounting* is similar in construction to those of the 8 cm and 10 cm German mortars, the recoil arrangements however being of a more substantial nature.

(iii) *The spigot* consists of a drawn steel tube reduced at its lower end and screw threaded externally to receive the supporting arm and

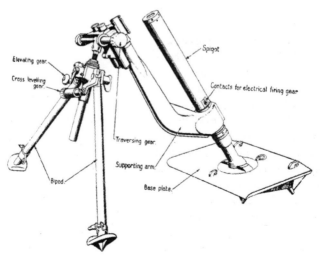

Fig 17—20 cm Spigot Mortar

base piece. It is bored transversely at its lower end to receive contact pieces and insulation for the electrical firing gear.

A T-shaped contact tube extends from these up the inside of the spigot, and is maintained centrally by an insulating spacing washer at the front end.

The front end of the spigot is closed by a screw plug, which is bored centrally to house a contact plug and insulating bushes, and also houses the firing needle and spring. The front face is prepared with an undercut groove to form a bayonet joint when the cartridge is placed in position.

(iv)   *The base piece* screws on to the spigot and is formed with a ball at the rear end to engage in the socket of the base plate.

(v)   *The supporting arm* is tubular and elbow shaped. The rear end is formed with a boss which is bored to receive the spigot, the front end is solid and is screw-threaded to receive a collar for positioning in the cradle.

(d)   *Ammunition*

(i)   20 *cm HE bomb* 40 (20 *cm Wurfgranate* 40) (Fig 18)

This is a nose fuzed bomb fitted with a tubular tail having eight stabilizing fins. The large proportion of explosive: to the total weight of bomb will produce considerable blast effect.

Details are as follows:—

Maximum diameter of bomb	7·79 in
Length of bomb (without fuze or tail)	10·63 in
Overall length of bomb	31·26 in
Weight of bomb filled	46¾ lb
Weight of filling	15 lb

(ii)   20 *cm smoke bomb* 40 (20 *cm Wurfgranate* 40)

No detailed information on this bomb is available at present, though it is probably of similar dimensions to the HE bomb but containing a smoke composition filling with an HE burster. The letters "Nb" will probably be found stencilled on the bomb casing.

(iii)   *Propellant charges*

There are three charges weighing respectively 540, 370, and 185 grains.

These are contained in a steel propellant case fitted with an electric primer, which is attached to the face of the spigot before the bomb is loaded.

On firing, the case separates, the upper part leaving the spigot with the bomb.

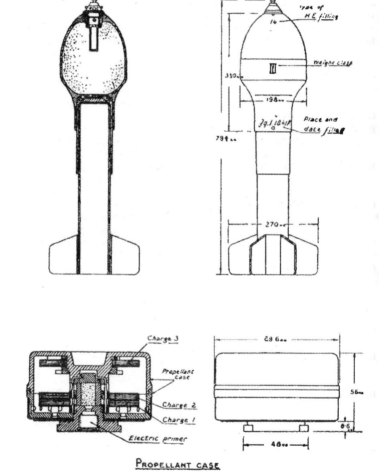

Fig 18—20 cm Spigot Mortar Bomb 40

APPENDIX A

INTERCHANGEABILITY OF BRITISH, GERMAN AND ITALIAN 2-IN AND 3-IN MORTAR AMMUNITION

Mortar	Bomb	Whether suitable	Remarks
British 2 in	German 5 cm (2 lb)	Yes	Average loss in range of 162·5 yards. Utility restricted to angles of elevation on either scale giving readings between 525 and 400 yards.
German 5 cm	British 2 in (2 lb)	No	Will not load.
British 3 in	German 8 cm (7¾ lb)	No	Can only be fired if strikers pipped or striker clips fitted.
British 3 in	Italian 81 mm (7¼ lb & 15 lb)	Yes	Lower MV and shorter maximum range than with Italian mortar.
German 8 cm	British 3 in (10 lb)	No	Can only be fired if adaptor is fitted to German mortar lengthening the striker stud.
German 8 cm	Italian 81 mm (7¼ lb & 15 lb)	Yes	Trials to determine whether German mortar will stand up to higher Italian charges not yet carried out. Can be safely fired at ranges up to 2,600 yards.
Italian 81 mm.	British 3 in (10 lb)	No	Needle disc clip fouls the striker housing and prevents a clean strike.
Italian 81 mm	German 8 cm (7¾ lb)	Yes	Recommended limits of QE: 45° and 80°. Ranges realized: 45°, 2,300 yards; 80°, 900 yards.

APPENDIX B
RANGE TABLE FOR 8 CM MORTAR

Charge I Range (yards)	Charge I Elevation (mils)	Charge II Range (yards)	Charge II Elevation (mils)	Charge III Range (yards)	Charge III Elevation (mils)	Charge IV Range (yards)	Charge IV Elevation (mils)	Charge V Range (yards)	Charge V Elevation (mils)
66	1545	328	1447	656	1388	1203	1289	1640	1255
100	1515	350	1435	700	1373	1250	1275	1650	1253
150	1471	400	1410	750	1354	1300	1260	1700	1240
200	1428	450	1386	800	1337	1350	1244	1750	1227
250	1381	500	1361	850	1318	1400	1228	1800	1214
300	1334	550	1335	900	1300	1450	1211	1850	1200
350	1282	600	1308	950	1280	1500	1195	1900	1187
400	1229	650	1278	1000	1261	1550	1177	1950	1172
450	1170	700	1250	1050	1241	1600	1158	2000	1157
500	1098	750	1220	1100	1219	1650	1138	2050	1142
550	1010	800	1188	1150	1196	1700	1118	2100	1125
591	891	850	1154	1200	1175	1750	1097	2150	1105
		900	1116	1250	1149	1800	1074	2200	1096
		950	1074	1300	1124	1850	1050	2250	1075
		1000	1023	1350	1096	1900	1023	2300	1055
		1050	956	1400	1066	1950	993	2350	1034
		1094	874	1450	1033	2000	956	2400	1011
				1500	994	2050	910	2450	985
				1550	949	2078	869	2500	957
				1597	881			2550	920
								2600	861
								2625	800

CHAPTER 8
Company Officer's Handbook, 1944

The US Military Intelligence Division *Company Officer's Handbook of the German Army* (Special Series 22) of March 1944 is a particularly significant manual for a number of reasons. Perhaps most importantly, and despite 'restricted' classification, this volume was issued right down to the level of the US company commander, in the United States, Europe, the Caribbean and elsewhere. It was therefore likely to be the volume of first recourse for an American unit, and the nub of what an officer knew about his enemy – and, apart from his own previous experience, what he could tell his men. The *Company Officer's Handbook* was also significant in its timing, for in March 1944 it was the last comprehensive effort to inform the troops before D-Day. It is therefore likely to be a decent reflection of the state of knowledge of the soldier on the beaches of Omaha and Utah, or at least of those who had been dedicated in their training or reading.

The volume begins with neither dry tabular information nor a history lesson but a summation of German offensive tactics. This was a good idea because this was almost certainly what a lazy reader needed to know, particularly in an emergency, and what the average officer was most likely to find interesting. Naturally enough defence followed offence, and subsequent chapters also covered the use of support weapons, and weapons in general.

What was included here was a veritable catalogue of the things sent to tribulate the GI in Normandy: the machine guns MG 34 and MG 42, rocket projectors such as the *Nebelwerfer*, the full gamut of howitzers and anti-tank guns, including the '88', and tanks up to and including the Panther and Tiger. Mines were included, such as the infamous 'bouncing Betty', but not so comprehensively since the reader was referred elsewhere for information on types made with wood and concrete. This may have been something of a lacuna since these, as well as those made of glass, were both fiendishly injurious and difficult to detect.

Section V covered the 'Combat Team': this was a particularly significant idea since the German Army had a long-standing tradition of forming such *Kampfgruppen* ('battle groups') to suit the task at hand. As the *Company Officer's Handbook* explained, this was a typical example of the 'high degree of flexibility' characteristic of the German organisation. Frequently such battle groups were known by the name of the commander, and mixed tank and infantry elements. In a typical case, such a group could include an entire infantry regiment alongside two tank battalions, four batteries of different sorts of artillery, two anti-tank companies and a company of engineers. Sometimes combat teams were a result of necessity rather than planning, and in Sicily, for example, it was not unknown for Italian troops to be included in a joint battle group.

The remainder of the *Company Officer's Handbook* returns to more familiar territory, with tables of strength and organisation and explanations of German military symbols. Tedious though these may have appeared, their inclusion was extremely welcome since an American unit capturing an enemy map, particularly one annotated with the positions of German defence works and batteries, would soon be able to work out the well-protected areas, or perhaps more importantly, avoid machine-gun bunkers and mine fields. Extracted here are the sections on German offensive tactics, which are arguably much more lucid and useful than the efforts encountered previously.

RESTRICTED
SPECIAL SERIES NO.22   31 MARCH 1944

COMPANY OFFICER'S HANDBOOK OF THE GERMAN ARMY PREPARED BY MILITARY INTELLIGENCE DIVISION WAR DEPARTMENT

SECTION I. OFFENSIVE PRINCIPLES

1. Attack

In the attack the Germans stress the principle that the enemy must be surrounded and destroyed. They believe that a strong, rapid enveloping attack can be decisive, provided that it really comes to grips with the enemy while he is pinned down by frontal pressure, which the Germans exert mainly by fire. The enveloping forces advance in depth in order to avoid being outflanked, the guiding principle being that all enveloping attacks ultimately become frontal. (See fig. 1.)

In all attacks a German commander will select a point of main effort (*Schwerpunkt*), where he will employ the bulk of his forces in order to force a decision. (See fig. 2.) A German maxim is—"A commander without a

Schwerpunkt is like a man without character." In selecting the point of main effort the Germans consider the following factors:

(a) Weaknesses in the enemy's defensive position.

(b) Suitability of the terrain, especially for tanks, and for cooperation of all arms.

(c) Approach routes.

(d) Possibilities for supporting fire, especially by artillery.

The Germans allot sectors and objectives to attacking units, but this does not mean that a unit must cover with troops the whole ground within its boundaries. The unit will choose the best line or lines of advance within its area and dispose its troops accordingly. The battalion making the assault at the point of main effort may be allotted a front of about 450 yards, while a battalion in another area may be assigned a front of 1,000 yards or more. In actual practice, unit frontages may vary considerably. During the Tunisian Campaign, General

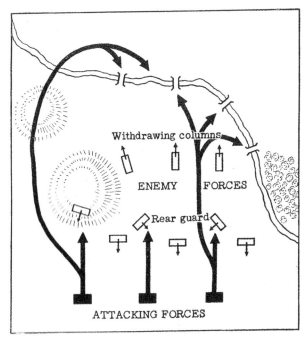

Fig 1—German enveloping tactics

Jürgen von Arnim, the German commander, stated that 1½ battalions might well attack on a front of 2,000 yards.

An attack on a narrow front, according to German doctrine, must have sufficient forces at its disposal to widen a penetration, maintain its impetus, and protect the flanks of the penetration. Once it is launched, the attack must drive straight to its objective, regardless of opposition. The Germans maintain that it is wrong for the foremost elements of the attacking forces to turn aside to deal with threats to their flanks. This is a task which is assigned to the troops that follow.

An effort is made by the Germans to push a break-through sufficiently deep to prevent the enemy from establishing new positions in the rear. The attacking forces attempt to reduce individual enemy positions by encircling and isolating them. They do not consider a break-through successful until they capture the enemy's artillery positions; usually this is the special task of tanks.

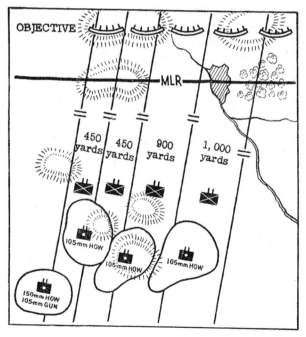

Fig 2—German Schwerpunkt: frontages and objective

Where enemy resistance weakens at any point, all available fire and forces are concentrated to ensure the success of the break-through. The artillery is kept well forward.

The Germans regard their self-propelled assault guns as decisive weapons which are employed particularly at the point of main effort. In cooperation with infantry, they facilitate the penetration and break-through with a minimum of casualties. These weapons, the Germans believe, complement artillery fire by their ability to follow the infantry right up to an objective. Their use for small actions before an attack is forbidden so as not to betray their presence. Surprise is sought by bringing them into position by night and camouflaging their assembly area. Used primarily to neutralize enemy support weapons at short ranges over open sights, assault guns are employed in concentrations; to employ them singly or in comparatively small number is frowned upon by the Germans.

German assault guns advance with or just behind the infantry; they never go ahead of the infantry. When an objective is reached, the assault guns do not remain with the infantry while the position is being consolidated but retire about 1,000 yards to await further assignment. It is a German principle that assault guns must always have close protection from the infantry which they are supporting.

Other characteristic features of German tactics in the attack are as follows:

(a) Some of the motorized supporting weapons are held back to exploit a success, to support a further advance, or to build up strength at the point of main effort.

(b) Smoke is used liberally, particularly to screen the flanks of an attacking force.

(c) Assault detachments, including engineers equipped with explosive charges and flame throwers, are used against strongly prepared defensive positions. Fire support for such detachments is heavy and carefully planned.

(d) Antitank guns of all calibers are employed, sometimes singly, against fixed positions and concrete emplacements.

(e) Small groups of riflemen with automatic weapons will infiltrate enemy positions and work around the flanks and rear of an enemy force in an effort to give the impression that it is surrounded. (See fig. 3.) In open warfare, reconnaissance details may be used for this purpose. Small groups may also infiltrate a position at night and open fire from the rear at dawn as a preliminary to an attack. Thus they attempt to cause confusion and to create the impression that the defenders are surrounded.

(f) Tanks tow or carry heavily armed infantry and engineers into combat in order to organize and hold positions in captured terrain, or to neutralize antitank defenses. Tanks may also be used to tow antitank guns.

2. Infantry and Tanks

Usually German tanks do not operate independently, but are employed in combat teams in cooperation with infantry, field and antitank artillery, and engineers. In the operations of armored divisions, tank units and panzer grenadiers (armored infantry) are combined and fight as a unified force. In an infantry-tank attack the Germans transport the infantry into battle on tanks or in troop-carrying vehicles in order to protect the infantry and to increase its speed. The infantry leaves the vehicles at the last possible moment, and goes into action mainly with light automatic weapons.

Before making a decision on the respective tasks of infantry and armored units, the commander of a combined force employs reconnaissance elements which differ from those used by an infantry commander in that they have greater fire power, speed, and mobility; he uses more armored cars and motorcycles, and supports them with a few tanks when necessary.

The Germans usually form combat teams of all arms whenever rapid deployment for a meeting engagement is expected. An advance guard consisting of panzer grenadiers, tanks, and antitank weapons moves ahead as a screen to cover the deployment of a combat team. If the terrain over which the attack is to be made is a natural tank obstacle, or if it is protected by antitank mine fields and ditches covered by fire, detachments of motorized infantry and engineers, perhaps with tank support, will clear a path for the main body of tanks.

In open country the Germans are prone to attack hard and fast in order to capture a commanding feature, which, because of its tactical importance, the enemy cannot afford to lose, thus compelling the enemy to counterattack at all costs. Once in possession of the feature, strong supporting artillery (including antitank and antiaircraft-antitank weapons) occupies forward positions, and the

Fig 3—German infantry firing automatic weapons. (The soldier at the left
is the sergeant commanding a squad of which the light machine gun is part.
Firing next to him is the lieutenant leading the platoon. Under cover of the
house is number 2 of the crew, with ammunition box in front of him.)

tanks withdraw to the rear of the artillery. Enemy armored vehicles and troops
which may counterattack are then confronted at once by a strong artillery
screen.

The Germans generally avoid tank-versus-tank actions, and adhere to the
principle that the task of the tanks is to break through and help to destroy
infantry, not necessarily to seek out and destroy enemy tanks. Destruction of
tanks is a mission assigned mainly to antitank units.

The Germans stress the need for the concentrated employment of the whole
available tank force, except necessary reserves, at the decisive place and time.
The tank force will try to penetrate to the enemy's lines of communication, and
the infantry will mop up. The attack normally proceeds in three waves. The
first wave thrusts to the enemy's artillery positions. The second wave provides
covering fire for the first wave, and then attacks the enemy's infantry position,
preceded, accompanied, or followed by part of (he panzer grenadiers, who
dismount from their combat vehicles as close as possible to the point where
they must engage the enemy. (See fig. 4.) The objectives of the second wave
are the enemy's antitank defenses and infantry positions, which are attacked

with high-explosive and machine-gun fire. The third wave, accompanied by the remainder of the panzer grenadiers, mops up.

The introduction of the heavy tank (*Pz.Kpfw. Tiger*) has led to a modification of German tactics, and reports from the Eastern Front indicate that *Tiger* tanks were sometimes used there in an independent role. The *Tiger* tank has been employed mainly to provide support for light and medium tanks. In one action in the Tunisian Campaign, however, lighter tanks formed the spearhead of an attack, but when Allied tanks came within range, the lighter German tanks deployed to the flanks and the *Tiger* tanks engaged.

In one attack in Russia. *Tiger* tanks were reported to have been used to obtain a battering-ram effect in an attack in the Byelgorod–Orel sector. A force of 20 to 30 *Tiger* tanks led the attack, followed by 40 to 60 self-propelled guns. Behind the guns were German light and medium tanks and some Czech light tanks used as mounts for guns of approximately 75-mm caliber. German light and medium tanks were also used to cover the flanks.

Fig 4—Panzer grenadiers going into combat direct from armored personnel carriers. (The near half-track vehicle mounts a light machine gun; the far one, a 37-mm antitank gun.)

3. Town and Street Fighting

In attacking a town or village, the Germans will employ flanking and encircling tactics (see fig. 5); one of their primary missions is to cut off water, electricity, and gas supplies. While carrying out the flanking maneuver, the Germans will endeavor to pin down the defenders with heavy artillery fire.

If a direct assault must be made on the town, the Germans favor laying heavy supporting fire on the forward edge of the community, especially on detached groups of buildings and isolated houses. The assaulting troops most likely will be divided into a number of columns and make a series of coordinated parallel attacks. Attacks from opposite directions and conflicting angles are avoided on the ground that they lead to confusion and to firing on friendly troops.

The columns will be subdivided into assault groups and mop-up groups. Assault detachments of engineers equipped with demolition equipment,

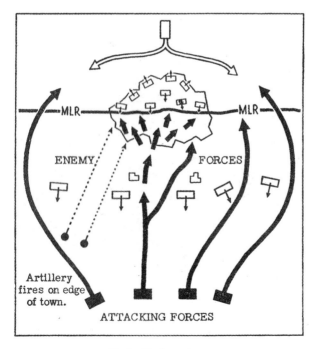

Fig 5—Attack on a town

flame throwers, and grenades, may accompany the infantry. The advance through the town is likely to be made in bounds measured in terms of one or a few streets; after each bound the troops re-form and proceed to new objectives. The Germans avoid the streets as much as possible and infiltrate simultaneously through back yards and over roofs, attempting to seize all high ground.

If it is necessary for them to advance through streets, the Germans move in two files, one on each side of the thoroughfare. The left side is preferred, as it is more advantageous for firing right-handed from doorways. Consideration is given to the problem of fighting against defenders organized not only in depth but also in height. Consequently the men, from front to rear, will be given specific assignments to watch the roofs, the various floors of buildings, and cellar windows. Side streets are blocked immediately, and at night searchlights are kept ready to illuminate roofs. The Germans endeavor to keep constant contact with the artillery, and single light guns may accompany the infantry in order to engage points of resistance with direct fire. Extensive use also is made of rocket weapons and mortars.

When a section of a town is captured, the Germans close up all side streets leading from the occupied area, block all exits of houses, and then begin a house-to-house search with details assigned to specific tasks, such as mopping up roofs, attics, basements, court-yards, and staircases. Cellars and attics are occupied first in organizing for defense.

4. Reconnaissance

a. General

In the German Army, normal reconnaissance is carried out by the division reconnaissance battalion. Reconnaissance patrols arc likely to be mixed, and may include cyclists, motorcyclists, cavalry, or armnred cars, depending on the type of division, and may be strongly reinforced with mobile close-support, and antitank weapons to enable them to cope with special situations. A relatively large number of antitank guns, which are likely to be self-propelled, are allotted to reconnaissance forces; this is also true of advance guards, in which the antitank guns are placed well forward.

The importance of reconnaissance was stressed by General Jürgen von Arnim, the German commander in the Tunisian Campaign, in a general order.

He said: "For correct handling of troops it is indispensable to know about the enemy. If one does not, one runs blindly into enemy fire. Therefore— reconnaissance and again reconnaissance! It must be carried out by sectors, from ridge to ridge (including reconnaissance of future artillery observation posts), in exactly the same way as the attack—to ensure that the supporting weapons follow up in time."

b. Armored Reconnaissance

The mission of the reconnaissance battalions of armored and motorized divisions, which have comparatively high fire power, is to make contact with the enemy and obtain information on his strength, assembly areas, approach routes, and movements. Contact is usually made frontally, and is shifted around the flanks and rear as enemy resistance stiffens and information is gained. Heavy engagements are avoided, but armored-car patrols are prepared to light for necessary information. (See fig. 6.)

The Germans are likely to employ patrols of eight-wheeled armored cars mounting 75-mm tank guns (a typical patrol generally consists of two such cars), in order to obtain mobility and fire power. Light patrols, equipped with

Fig 6—Reconnaissance patrol of an SS division. (The patrol consists of motorcyclists and eight-wheeled armored cars. The motorcyclists are armed with rifles, submachine guns, and light machine guns.)

three four-wheeled armored cars or with armored half-tracks, are employed on short-range tasks, liaison missions, and observation; they seldom attempt to fight. Patrols may be reinforced with engineers and motorcyclists to deal with road blocks and demolitions. Rifle companies belonging to the reconnaissance battalion may be attached to break minor enemy resistance. The fire of their infantry guns may be supplemented by attached field artillery. Tanks are not likely to be furnished as support, because they are too noisy and slow.

Armored reconnaissance patrols carry out missions up to 60 miles deep. On the march, they proceed 40 to 60 miles in advance of the main body, operating on the prongs of a **Y** on a front of some 20 miles.

Each patrol (in the case of a three-car patrol) marches with a radio car in the rear. Commanding features are approached slowly, and, following careful scrutiny, are rapidly passed. Parallel roads are covered successively. In scouting a wood, the leading car will drive towards the edge, halt briefly to observe, and then drive off rapidly. By this ruse the Germans attempt to draw fire which will disclose the enemy positions. At road blocks, the leading car will open fire. If fire is not returned, men will dismount and go forward to attach long tow ropes to the road block. When necessary, men will dismount and proceed with submachine guns to reconnoiter on foot. Dismounted men are covered by the car's guns. If obstacles prove formidable, or are defended by antitank guns, patrols will report by radio. Pending orders, they will seek a detour. The commander may order the patrol either to by-pass the obstacle or to await reinforcement.

5. Patrols

When German forces were in close contact with Allied forces during the Tunisian Campaign, their patrols did not, as a rule, operate offensively by night, nor did they reconnoiter as deeply as Allied patrols. Many of the German patrols consisted of 30 to 40 men; they moved in close formation at night, making themselves vulnerable to ambush. Rather than make long, deep patrols, the Germans preferred to establish an advanced base from which further patrols were sent out. On the other hand, they made a practice of taking up positions early at night in no-man's land in efforts to ambush Allied patrols.

Of the offensive patrols that were undertaken virtually all were made by the Hermann Göring Jäger Regiment. Sometimes three men went forward to reconnoiter while the main body of the patrol waited under cover. The technique was first to make a penetration into a position and then to employ grenades and light machine guns. In the resulting confusion the Germans would attempt to withdraw with prisoners.

Daylight offensive patrols were exceptional, but the striking feature of one such raid was its evidently careful planning. The raid was made by a platoon of the Hermann Göring Jäger Regiment, divided into a fire party, with light machine guns and grenades; an assault party, with grenades and fixed bayonets; and a demolition party. The timing was perfect, no signals were used, and the raid appeared to have been rehearsed. The three parties attacked successively from three directions and the demolition group succeeded in damaging a field gun.

6. Meeting engagement

A German commander will normally avoid a meeting engagement unless he feels that his troops and leadership are superior to the enemy's (this does not necessarily mean numerical superiority), or unless the loss of time in mounting a deliberate attack would result in a sacrifice of terrain which he cannot afford to lose. The Germans teach that it is essential to make sound tactical decisions in the initial stages of a meeting engagement and that mistakes cannot be rectified, but they believe that the worst mistake is hesitation.

When the Germans do commit themselves to a meeting engagement, they will deploy the main body immediately. They proceed on the principle that time lost in such circumstances cannot be regained, and, therefore, they deem it wrong to lose time in the hope of clarifying the situation. Their normal tactics then would be to coordinate a frontal assault of the advance guard with one or more enveloping attacks by the main body. Great emphasis is laid on obtaining superiority in the fire fight by a liberal allotment of supporting weapons.

7. Deployment

The Germans carry out deployment in two stages. They call the first stage *Entfaltung,* or "shaking out," which is equivalent to the development of a march column according to U. S. procedure. In the first stage (fig. 7(1)), an infantry regiment normally deploys down to battalions, although the procedure may go down to companies if a high state of preparedness is necessary. The second stage (fig. 7(2)), called *Entwicklung,* is deployment in detail, which is the final action of the company extending itself down to platoons and squads.

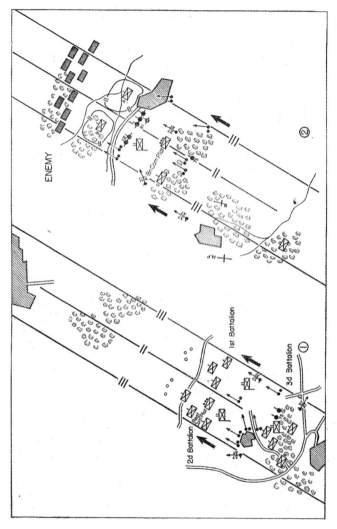

Fig 7—Deployment of a German Infantry regiment:
(1) first stage (deployment by battalions);
(2) second stage (deployment in detail).

A factor considered by the Germans in determining when to deploy is the additional physical strain placed on men when they march cross-country.

Features of the first stage of deployment are as follows:

(a) Companies retain their combat vehicles until their weapons and equipment arrive at the off-carrier position, which is located as far forward as the situation permits.

(b) The Germans often place only one company forward, the main strength of the battalion being kept under control of the battalion commander as long as possible so that he may employ it in the most advantageous direction for attack.

(c) If the condition of the terrain and enemy fire cause a change of intervals between units, the normal intervals are resumed as soon as possible.

(d) Support weapons are used to cover the "shaking out" phase of deployment and the subsequent advance, the weapons being kept within the march column between the companies or behind the battalion.

(e) After the first stage of deployment has been carried out, the leading elements of the battalion may be ordered to seize important tactical features.

(f) When deploying by night or in woods, a careful reconnaissance is made, routes are marked, and strong protection is placed forward. Intervals between units are shorter.

(g) After the first stage of deployment has been completed, the battalion commander marches with the leading elements and will normally send reconnaissance patrols ahead or reconnoiter the enemy position himself. The commanders of support weapons accompany him, reconnoitering for firing positions.

Features of the second stage of deployment are as follows:

(a) The companies deploy in depth as soon as they come within range of artillery fire. An advance in columns of files is considered desirable because it affords a small target and the company is easier to control, but before adopting this formation the danger of enfilading fire is weighed.

(b) If enemy fire and difficult terrain necessitate further deployment, the companies disperse in depth by sections. Reserves and support weapons also adopt open formations, but they remain far enough behind to avoid coming under the fire directed at the leading elements.

(c) When the rifle companies are deployed, they exploit all possible cover as they advance, employing single-file or column-of-file formations with irregular intervals. The leading elements are not extended until they are to engage in a fire fight. The elements that follow continue advancing in file.

An American soldier with, left, the MG 42, and, right, the 'Sturmgewehr' or 'assault rifle'. Firing an intermediate sized 7.92 mm cartridge from a 30 round magazine the Sturmgewehr could be used in full automatic mode on the move, but was much more accurate than a sub machine gun. Total production of all versions of this weapon totalled a little under half a million.

CHAPTER 9
Handbook of the German Army, 1945

Well before June 1944, thought was given as to how the Allies would exploit the intelligence opportunities presented by landings in Europe. In the British instance, authorisation was given for the formation of a 'Special Intelligence Unit' of Navy, Army and Airforce personnel as early as 1942; one of its key organisers was Commander Ian Fleming, now better known as the anothor of the James Bond novels. The formation acted in co-operation with the Intelligence Corps Field Security sections, and information was passed back from North Africa and Greece. Before the end of 1943 the unit was operating in the guise of a 'Commando' under the innocuous designation '30 Assault Unit'. Its task was to advance ahead of Allied forces, or to infiltrate and seize intelligence. Before D-Day a special Allied 'T-Force' of US and British personnel was established for the 'exploitation of scientific and industrial targets'. Though begun small, this would eventually employ several thousand people. New evidence was thus added to existing knowledge to update information fed into Allied equipment programmes and given to fighting troops.

The total amount of material processed by Allied intelligence increased exponentially with time so that the biggest problem in the latter part of the war was no longer collecting enough, but digesting what was gathered. Italy, difficult early in the war, opened up rapidly as a result of its invasion. Once Italy joined the Allies its military secret service ('SIM') began to pass on knowledge of the Germans. Greece and Turkey remained active areas of intelligence operations. Despite early setbacks, British intelligence behind enemy lines in the Netherlands grew to a network of three hundred agents and assistants. In Scandinavia, British intelligence doubled its output by October 1944, the majority of its seven hundred reports per month being 'Armed Forces Information'. French networks, already active, were galvanised by expectation, then by the reality of cross-Channel invasion and the planting of new teams behind the battlefront. The breakout from Normandy at the end of July led to the overrunning and the capture of large numbers of enemy troops and their equipment.

Arguably the last word on the matter of the German Army of the Second World War was the magisterial *Handbook on German Military Forces*, US War Department Technical Manual TM-E 30-451, of 15 March 1945. In its original form, and despite being billed as permanent and comprehensive, this was a type of 'part work' of ten chapters, being issued in a 'loose leaf format' to 'facilitate revision'. While the *Handbook on German Military Forces* could not really claim to contain everything, its coverage was impressive and included not just the Army but the Air Force, a fair smattering of information on recruitment, the SS and other organisations, and tactics. Remarkably the *Handbook* claimed to include material gathered as recently as 15 February 1945.

Perhaps the greatest pity was that this remarkable volume can have seen relatively little practical use, and have had few of the envisioned revisions added for the war in Europe ended just weeks after its publication. The brief extracts included here target material not covered in the documents previously quoted: namely the German soldier of 1945; the various categories of officers and personnel; and the types of, and changes to, infantry divisions. The illustrations in this chapter are from the pages of the *Handbook*.

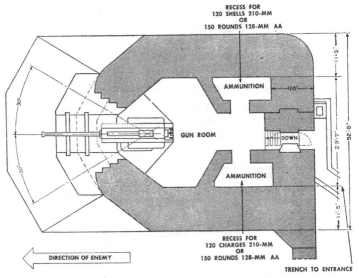

A typical German gun casemate, type 685. The handbook featured a
range of the standard patterns. By 1945 the Allies had copious experience
of enemy reinforced concrete designs from the Atlantic Wall and other
theatres. Casemates for large guns featured walls two metres thick.

The four-wheeled Sd Kfz 222 light armoured car was an improved version
of the 221 model produced from 1935 to 1940. The 222 weighed 5 tons and
from 1942 had a maximum frontal armour of 30 mm. Maximum road speed was
85 km/h. The usual armament was a 2 cm automatic gun and an MG 34.

The Büssing-NAG Sd Kfz 232 was one of a family of eight-wheeled
heavy armoured cars first conceived in the mid-1930s. Manufactured
from 1939 to 1942, they had both steering and drive to all eight wheels,
and two sets of controls allowing for swift advance and reverse.

VEHICLE FOR DECONTAMINATION OF PERSONNEL
(Kfz. 92)

The Kfz 92 decontamination truck was based on a Henschel type 33 chassis.
In its intended role it carried anti-gas suits and other kit for the crew, hose reels,
showering equipment and Losantin powder to decontaminate personnel.

Men of the South Staffordshire Regiment with a selection of German weapons.
Left: the 88mm Racketen Panzerbuchse. Held by the Sergeant, centre: two
different models of the Panzerfaust single shot anti tank weapon. *Right*: mines
and grenades, including the plate shaped 'Teller' anti tank mine, the 'bouncing
betty' anti personnel mine, and the hand thrown 'stick' and 'egg' grenades.

SECTION II. THE GERMAN SOLDIER

1. Fanatic or Weakling?

The German soldier who faces the Allies on the home fronts in 1945 is a very
different type from the members of the Army of 1939 which Hitler called "an Army
such as the world has never seen". The German soldier is one of several different
types depending on whether he is a veteran of 4 or 5 years, or a new recruit. The
veteran of many fronts and many retreats is a prematurely aged, war weary cynic,
either discouraged and disillusioned or too stupefied to have any thought of his
own. Yet he is a seasoned campaigner, most likely a noncommissioned officer,
and performs his duties with the highest degree of efficiency.

The new recruit, except in some crack *SS* units, is either too young or too
old and often in poor health.

He has been poorly trained for lack of time but, if too young, he makes up for
this by a fanaticism bordering on madness. If too old, he is driven by the fear of
what his propagandists have told him will happen to the Fatherland in case of an

Allied victory, and even more by the fear of what he has been told will happen to him and his family if he does not carry out orders exactly as given. Thus even the old and sick perform, to a certain point, with the courage of despair.

The German High Command has been particularly successful in placing the various types of men where they best fit, and in selecting those to serve as cannon fodder, who are told to hold out to the last man, while every effort is made to preserve the elite units, which now are almost entirely part of the *Waffen-SS*. The German soldier in these units is in a preferred category and is the backbone of the German Armed Forces. He is pledged never to surrender and has no moral code except allegiance to his organization. There is no limit to his ruthlessness.

The mentality of the German soldier of 1945 is the final result of that policy of militarism which, even in the 19th century, caused a famous German general to recommend that soldiers should be trained to ask of their superiors: "Master, order us where we may die."

2. Manpower Problems

a. Annual Class System. When Hitler reintroduced general conscription in 1935, the greatest possible care was taken to create a strong military force without disrupting the economic life of the nation. Men were registered by annual classes and during the years before the war those of the older classes were called only in small groups to attend training exercises of limited duration. Even for the younger classes, all feasible arrangements were made for the deferment of students and of those engaged in necessary occupations. Men accepted for active service were called to the colors by individual letter rather than by public announcement for their annual class. This system was continued in the gradual mobilization which preceded the outbreak of the war in such a way that the wartime Army could be built up organically and the normal course of life was not seriously upset.

b. War Developments. As long as the war was conducted on a limited scale, the Armed Forces were very liberal in granting occupational and medical discharges. As the war progressed and grew in scope and casualties mounted, it became necessary to recall many of these men and eventually to reach increasingly into both the older and the younger age groups.

After Germany changed from the offensive to the defensive in 1943, it became both possible and necessary to transfer an increasing number of Air Force and naval personnel to the Army, to enforce "voluntary" enlistment in the *Waffen-SS,* and to commit line-of-communication units to regular combat not only against partisans but against regular enemy forces.

The increasingly heavy losses of the Russian campaign forced Hitler to cancel his order exempting "last sons" of decimated families and fathers of large families from front-line combat duty. Prisons and concentration camps were combed out for men who could be used in penal combat units with the inducement of possible later reinstatement of their civic rights.

Although a "total mobilization" was carried out in the spring of 1943, after Stalingrad, it became necessary by the end of that year to lower the physical classification standards drastically and to register men up to 60 years of age for military service. Even men with severe stomach ailments were drafted into special-diet battalions. During the summer of 1944, civilian occupations were reduced to an absolutely necessary minimum. Finally, the remaining male civilians from 16 to 60 were made liable for home defense combat service in the *"Volkssturm"* and even Hitler Youth boys and girls were called up as auxiliaries.

Along with these measures there went a continuous reorganization of combat as well as administrative units for the purpose of increasing efficiency and saving personnel.

The strength of divisions was lowered while their firepower was increased and their components were made more flexible. Severe comb-outs were made among rear-area personnel and technical specialists. The strongest possible measures were introduced against waste of manpower, inefficiency, and desertions, particularly after the Army was brought under the ever increasing control of the *SS,* in the summer and autumn of 1944.

After the Allied breakthrough in France, Himmler was appointed Commander of the Replacement Army and as such made the *Waffen-SS* the backbone of German national defense. Whole units of the Air Force and Navy were taken over and trained by the *Waffen-SS* and then distributed among depleted field units. The organization and employment of the *Volkssturm* is under Himmler's direct control.

The complicated record system of the Armed Forces was maintained in principle but streamlined for the sake of saving manpower.

c. Foreign Elements. (1) *Original policy.* In their attempts to solve their ever acute manpower problems, the Germans have not neglected to make the fullest possible use of foreign elements for almost every conceivable purpose and by almost every conceivable method. Originally, great stress was laid on keeping the Armed Forces nationally "pure". Jews and Gypsies were excluded from military service. Foreign volunteers were not welcomed. Germans residing abroad and possessing either German or dual citizenship were rounded up through the German consulates from 1937 on. When Germany set out to invade other countries, beginning with Austria, only the inhabitants of these countries who were held to be of German or related blood became liable to German military service; the Czech minority in Austria, for example, was exempted.

(2) *Recruiting of foreigners.* With the invasion of Russia in June 1941, German propagandists set themselves to the task of changing the whole aspect of the war from a national German affair to a "European war of liberation from Communism". In this way the Nazis were able to obtain a considerable number of volunteers from occupied and even neutral countries, who were organized in combat units of their own in German uniforms and under German training. The original policy was to incorporate racially related "Germanic" people, such as the Dutch and Scandinavians, into the *Waffen-SS* and non-Germanic people such as the Croats into the Army. When the failures in Russia and other increasing difficulties began to affect the morale of the foreigners, their "voluntary recruitment" became more and more a matter of compulsion and their service in separate national units had to be brought under more rigid supervision. The organization of such units, therefore, was turned over in increasing measure to the *Waffen-SS*. even in the case of racially non-Germanic elements.

At the same time, it became necessary for the Army to fill its own depleted German units by adding a certain percentage of foreign recruits. This was done partly by declaring the inhabitants of annexed territories, such as the Polish Corridor, to be "racial Germans" (*Volksdeutsche*), making them provisional German citizens subject to induction into the Armed Forces. A considerable source of manpower was Soviet prisoners of war of different national origins. Some of these were put into regular German units as "racial" Germans; others were employed in such units as "auxiliary volunteers". Separate national units also were created from Cossacks and from the numerous peoples who inhabit the Caucasus and Turkestan and are collectively referred to by the Germans as "Eastern Peoples" (*Ostvölker*). Every possible inducement has been used for the recruiting of foreigners, including their religion, as in the case of the Mohammedans in the Balkans. Only in the case of Jews and Gypsies was the original policy of exclusion not only upheld but extended during the war to include those of 50 per cent Jewish descent.

3. Duties and Rights of the Soldier

a. The Oath. Every German soldier, upon induction, is compelled to affirm his legally established military obligation by means of the following *oath* (vow, for atheists): *"I swear by God this holy oath* (I vow) that I will render unconditional obedience to the Führer of Germany and of her people, Adolf Hitler, the Supreme Commander of the Armed Forces, and that, as a brave soldier, I will be prepared to stake my life for this *oath* (vow) at any time."* If, because of an oversight, the oath has not been administered to a soldier, he is held to be in the same position as though he had sworn it; the oath is regarded only as the affirmation of an inherent legal duty.

b. Military Discipline. The German system of military discipline is rigorous, and excesses are severely punished. In principle, absolute and unquestioning obedience towards superiors is required. However, since the summer of 1944, when the Army came under the political influence of the Nazi Party, new orders were issued providing that disloyal superiors not only need not be obeyed but in emergencies may be liquidated by their own men. Officers who do not lead their men into combat or show other signs of cowardice or who, for any reason, mutilate themselves, are normally condemned to death. Divisional commanders and other high-ranking combat officers are specifically ordered to set an example of leadership in the front lines; this explains the high casualty rate among German generals.

Traditionally, German superior officers were addressed only indirectly, in the third person, as "Herr Major is absolutely right." Hitler, however, is addressed directly as "My Leader". Therefore, the Nazis made use of the direct form of address toward superior officers at first optional, then compulsory. Superior officers and noncommissioned officers are addressed as "Mr." (*Herr*) followed by their rank; in the *Waffen-SS,* however, only by their rank: *"Herr Leutnant!",* but *"Unterstürmführer!"*

Originally, a distinction was made between the regular military salute and the "German salutation" (*Deutscher Gruss*) which consists of saying "Heil Hitler!" with the right arm outstretched. In August 1944 the latter type of salute was made compulsory throughout. Everyone salutes his own superiors as well as others entitled to a salute according to the following general rules: Every officer is the superior of all lower-ranking officers and all enlisted men; every noncommissioned officer is the superior of all privates; every noncommissioned officer in one of the first three grades is the superior of lower-grade noncommissioned officers *in his own unit*. There is no general rank superiority otherwise among noncommissioned officers or among the various grades of privates; however, all members of the Armed Forces are obligated to "greet" one another as a matter of military etiquette.

Members of the Armed Forces are forbidden to associate with foreigners even if they are racially related; marriages between soldiers and non-German women are subject to approval, which is given only after a very thorough investigation; the offspring of such marriages are considered to be German. In the *Waffen-SS*, such marriages are entirely prohibited for German personnel.

Men who severely and repeatedly violate military discipline, but not to an extent that warrants a death sentence, are transferred to correction battalions for a probationary period and given arduous and dangerous assignments; if incorrigible, they are then turned over to the police for extreme punishment.

c. Preservation of Honor. Honor is considered the soldier's highest possession. Except in extreme cases, he may be given the opportunity to redeem himself for a dishonorable action by a heroic death in battle or, in milder cases, by exceptionally brave and meritorious service in the lowest grade of private to which he is reduced from his former rank. However, there also exists a rigid personal honor code for officers. Under its provisions, they are obligated to defend their own personal honor as well as the good name of their wives by every possible means and are held to account for violations committed by themselves or their wives. According to the German conception, special honor rules apply to officers and those civilians who are socially their equals. These rules provide in extreme cases for settlement by duel with pistols until one of the two parties is fully incapacitated. This is a leftover from feudal times; before Hitler's assumption of power, a half-hearted attempt was made to outlaw duelling by officers, but the penalties provided were light and did not carry moral stigma. It is significant that under Hitler, duelling of officers was legalized in cases where all efforts at settlement by an officers court of honor appointed by a regimental or higher commander fail; however, for duels between two officers, but not between an officer and a civilian, a decision must first be obtained from the Commander-in-Chief of the Army. Their medieval conception of honor has a strong influence on the mentality and actions of many German officers. An officer is obligated to react to deliberate insults instantaneously, in a positive and masterly fashion, and to protect other officers from becoming the object of public disgrace.

In the *SS*, "qualified" enlisted men (i.e. those who carry the dagger) are subject to the same honor rules as officers, being obligated to "defend their honor by force of arms".

4. Morale Factors

a. Relationship Between Officers and Men. The opening of the officer's career to the common German man of the people was a revolutionary change in the German social system brought about by Hitler. It has created an entirely different type of relationship among the ranks than existed in the armies of Imperial Germany.

No one can become an officer without being a certified Nazi, even if not a member of the Party, and without being considered capable of imbuing his men with the Nazi spirit. Thus, the social mingling between officers and men in off-duty hours, which has been encouraged by the Nazis to some extent, appears to have a strong propagandist purpose. A sincere personal interest of the officer in his men is encouraged, the all-important requirement being that he must have their confidence. In case of death, the soldier's next of kin receive their first notification through a personal letter from his company commander, which is handed to them by the local leader of the Nazi Party.

b. Politics in the Armed Forces. Traditionally, all German military personnel is barred from all political activities including the right to vote. Hitler, when introducing general conscription, maintained this tradition in order to obtain the full support of the military and decreed that membership in the Nazi Party and all political activities would be dormant during the period of any man's active service. In the later stages of the war, however, serious reverses and the increasing danger of sagging morale caused the official introduction of politics into the German Armed Forces. This occurred progressively from the latter part of 1943 on, by appointment of National-Socialist guidance officers (*NS-Führungs-offisiere*) on all staffs, the organization of political meetings, and other efforts at raising morale, as well as through the merciless terrorization of wavering officers and soldiers by the "strong men" of the *Waffen-SS*.

c. Awards. A very extended and clever use has been made of honorary titles for units, medals and awards for individual achievements, and commemorative decorations for participation in outstanding combat engagements. It is significant, for instance, that because the German is basically averse to hand-to-hand combat, the golden close-combat bar was created in 1944, which is bestowed by Hitler personally at his headquarters, as the highest honor offered the German soldier. Himmler shortly thereafter created the golden partisan-combat bar which he bestows personally at his headquarters. The requirements for winning either bar are extremely severe so that soldiers will do their utmost. Awards and decorations may be held to have acted as very important morale-builders for the German Armed Forces.

7. Categories of Officers and Other Personnel

a. Regular Officers (*aktive Offiziere*). The small corps of regular officers inherited by the Nazi regime from the pre-1935 German *Reichswehr* was substantially increased, before the war, by the recall of all suitable retired officers, the absorption of many police officers, and the creation of new officers from volunteer officer candidates and suitable noncommissioned officers and privates from the regular ranks. At the beginning of the war, suitable professional noncommissioned officers were given temporary officer ranks (as *"Kriegsoffiziere"*), which were made permanent in 1942.

Special categories of regular officers are medical officers (*Sanitätsoffiziere*), veterinary officers (*Veterinäroffiziere*), and ordnance officers (*Waffenoffiziere*, commonly designated as *Offiziere (W)*).

After 1934, a number of First World War officers were recalled, mostly in administrative positions, as supplementary officers (*Ergänzungsoffiziere*) and designated as *aktive Offiziere (E)*; the (E) has since been dropped and those who were qualified have been taken into the regular officer corps. Many officers who had been retired as "officers not in service" (*Offiziere ausser a.D.*) as well as many regular officers eligible for retirement were designated as subject to active service in recalled status "at the disposal of a branch of the Armed Forces (Army, Air Force, or Navy)" (*Offiziere zur Verfügung cines Wehrmachtteiles— z.V.*). Retired officers designated *z.V.* were normally not recalled to active service before mobilization, but a number of them were appointed in peacetime to fill certain open officer positions as "officers recalled to service." (*Offiziere zur Dienstleistung—z.D.*). During the war, the designation *z.D.* has been used for certain officers whose qualifications are in doubt and whose final status (regular or reserve) is not determined. The designation of regular officers subject to retirement as *z.V.* continues in wartime, which means that such officers, immediately upon their discharge as regular officers, are retained in active service in recalled status in any position in which they may be needed.

b. General Staff Corps Officers (*Generalstabsoffiziere, Offz.i.G.*). General Staff Corps officers are carefully selected and trained to represent the German General Staff Corps in both command and staff functions. On division staffs, as *"Ia"*, they hold the position of operational chiefs of staff, and as *"Ib"* they are chiefs of the rear echelon. In the higher echelons, the intelligence and training staff sections are likewise in the personal charge of General Staff Corps officers.

c. Reserve Officers (*Reserveoffiziere*). The nucleus of the reserve officer corps consists of conscripts who because of their qualifications and performance during their first year of service were accepted in peacetime as reserve officer aspirants (*Reserve-Offizier-Anwärter—R.O.A.*). received special training in platoon-leadership during their second year, and were designated reserve officers after their discharge and subsequent recall for a four-week exercise period with their old unit. Suitable professional noncommissioned officers were made reserve second lieutenants upon being discharged at the end of their contractual period.

In wartime, there cannot be any reserve officer candidates of the peacetime type, as conscripts are not being discharged upon completion of a compulsory two-year service period; instead, qualified volunteers and suitable conscripts from the ranks are designated as reserve officer applicants (*Reserve-Offizier-Bewerber—R.O.B.*).

Originally, there were two age groups of reserve officers, those of the reserve class under the age of 35, designated as *Offiziere der Reserve—O.d.R.*), and those of the *Landwehr* reserve class above 35, designated as *Offiziere der Landwehr—O.d.L.* Both types of officers, collectively, were called "officers in inactive status" (*Offiziere des Beurlaublenstandes—O.d.B.*). During the war, the designation O.d.L. has been eliminated, so that all reserve officers are *O.d.R.* as well as *O.d.B.*

d. Armed Forces Officials (*Wehrmachtbeamte*). Officials in administrative, legal, and technical service positions are a category peculiar to the German Armed Forces. They consist of civil service personnel performing functions with in the Armed Forces and are recruited, in part, from former professional noncommissioned officers who become military candidates for civil service (*Militäranwärter*) at the end of their 12-year contractual period of active military service. Until 1944, none of these officials were classified as soldiers, but certain groups have now been converted into officers in the Special Troop Service (*Truppensonderdienst—TDS*). These are the higher administrative officers (*Intendanten*) in ranks from captain to lieutenant general: the lower administrative officers (*Zahlmeister*) in the ranks of first and second lieutenant, and the judge advocates (*Richter*) in ranks from captain to lieutenant general. It was also made possible for reserve technical service officials to become reserve officers of the motor maintenance troops if qualified.

In addition to regular Armed Forces officials, there are the categories of reserve officials (*Beamte des Beurlaubtenstandes—B.d.B.,* also referred to as *B.d.R.*), officials in recalled status "at the disposal of the Army, etc." (*Beamte sur Verfügung—B.z.V.*), and officials appointed for the duration (*Beamte auf Kriegsdauer—B.o.K.*). These three categories are collectively referred to as supplementary Armed Forces officials (*Ergänzungswehrmachtbeamte*). Functionaries of the military administration in occupied areas (*Militäverwaltungsbeamte*) who are not civil service officials in peacetime are treated in the same manner as these three categories in matters of compensation.

e. Specialist Leaders. Certain positions in ranks from major to lieutenant and in all noncommissioned officer ranks except sergeant may be filled by specialists in foreign languages, propaganda work, and similar matters, who have been trained to fill such positions as "Specialist leader" (*Sonderführer*). They receive the pay applicable to the position they are holding, but only by virtue of their appointment to the temporary position and without the disciplinary powers vested in the rank.

f. Noncommissioned Officers (*Unteroffiziere*). Professional noncommissioned officers are under either a 12-year or a 4½-year service contract, except officer applicants, who are under contract for an indefinite period of service. Non-professionals are designated as reserve corporals, etc. (*Unteroffiziere*, etc., *d.R.*); the same applies if they are reserve officer candidates (*Fahnenjunker*, etc., *d.R.*).

g. Women Auxiliaries (*Helferinnen*). There are several women's auxiliary corps in the German Armed Forces, known as the corps of the headquarters auxiliaries (*Stabshelferinnen*); signal corps auxiliaries (*Nachrichtenhelferinnen*) of the Army, Air Force, *Waffen-SS,* and Navy; and antiaircraft auxiliaries (*Flakwaffenhelferinnen*) of the Air Force, All wear uniforms and are under military discipline, receiving free rations, quarters, and clothing. However, they are paid according to civil service rates and are not considered members of the Armed Forces. The ranks of their female leaders (*Führerinnen*) do not correspond to officer ranks. It is possible that they have been upgraded in status under recent total mobilization measures.

h. "Civilian" Soldiers (*Volkssturm*). In October 1944, all German male civilians from 16 to 60 were made liable to emergency defense service under the Armed Forces in a national militia known as the *"Volkssturm"*. They are distinguished by armbands and are stated to have military status. It is believed that they do not receive any service pay while in training but that they may be compensated when mobilized for combat away from their home area.

i. Other Armed Forces Personnel (*Wehrmachtgefolge*). A distinction must be made between members of the Armed Forces (*Wehrmachtangehörige*) who may be either soldiers or officials (*Beamte*), and persons employed by or attached to the Armed Forces (*Zugehörige zur Wehrmacht*), who are collectively referred to as Armed Forces auxiliaries (*Wehrmachtgefolge*). The women auxiliaries described above, as well as the numerous Party organizations when they operate with the Armed Forces, are in this general category.

2. Infantry Divisions

Despite the important role which has been played by specialized branches of the German Army, the infantry has been and remains today the foundation for most German operations.

a. Infantry Division, Old Type (*Infanteriedivision*) (Three Regiments of Three Battalions Each). Contrary to the American conception of a completely motorized infantry division, the German infantry divisions mostly have relied on horse-drawn vehicles for their transportation. In recent reorganizations the proportion of motorization in these types of divisions has decreased even more. Except for the reorganization of the infantry platoon from three to four squads after the Polish campaign in 1939, and the temporary increase in the number of horses in the divisions employed in Russia from 1941 to 1943, the German three-regiment, nine-battalion division remained unchanged for all practical purposes until the fall of 1943. This type of division probably will not be encountered any more; however, as it has been the basic type of German infantry division for a period of about 4 years, it is shown in Figures 7 and 8 and designated for explanatory purposes as the Infantry Division, Old Type.

b. Infantry Division, 1944 Type (*Infanterie-division n.A* later *Kriegestat 44*) (Three Regiments of Two Battalions Each). In October 1943 the Germans reorganized radically their infantry divisions in reducing the infantry regiments from three to two battalions, and the other divisional components were revised accordingly. In the remaining six infantry battalions the number of squads per rifle platoon was reduced from four to three, but without having much effect on the fire power of the division since the caliber of the mortars and antitank guns has been increased, and the number of machine guns kept unchanged. This type of division was designated Infantry Division, New Type (*Infanteriedivision n.A.*). This type of infantry division will not be discussed further here, as it soon was designated the Infantry Division, 1944 Type (*Infanterie-division Kriegestat 44*). This redesignation took place in May 1944 after the following additional economies were put into effect. The strength of the squad was reduced from ten to nine, the number of light machine guns per rifle company from 16 to 13, and the strength of the trains on all levels was reduced sharply. Figures 9 and 10 show the Infantry Division, 1944 Type, but newest regulations point towards a further reduction of the components of that type of division by approximately 10 per cent and the redesignation of the thus reorganized division as Infantry Division, Type 1945 (*Infanteriedivisions 45*). It has just been learned that all German infantry divisions are to be reorganized on the basis of the Infantry Division, Type 45, and that the organization and strength of that division are almost identical with those of the *Volks Grenadier* Division. (See subparagraph d below and Section VI, paragraph 2, subparagraph a (5).)

c. Infantry Division, Two Regiment Type (*Infanteriedivision*) (Two Regiments of Three Battalions Each). Independent of the various stages of organization of the three regiment infantry divisions, the Germans have formed, since the spring of 1941, a number of two-regiment, six-battalion, infantry divisions with weaker components and over-all reduced strength and fire power. The number of this type of divisions recently has been reduced by the reorganization of several into three-regiment divisions. We refer to this type of division as Infantry Division, Two-Regiment Type.

d. *Volks Grenadier* Division (*Volksgrena-dierdivision*) (Three Regiments of Two Battalions Each). In September 1944, after Heinrich Himmler, the Chief of the *SS,* the Police and the Minister of the Interior had become also the Chief of Army Equipment and Commander of the Replacement Training Army, a new type of infantry division, the "Peoples Infantry Division" (*Volks Grenadier* Division) was created. The political significance of this type of division lies in designating it: "the Peoples," and thus stressing the emergency of the Fatherland. As the members of the *Volks Grenadier* Division are reported to be interchangeable with the members of the *SS* divisions, it is believed that through their creation the influence of the *SS* on the Army has been strengthened. To increase the

Esprit de Corps of its members, supporting General Headquarters units also have been designated *Volks* Artillery Corps, *Volks* Engineer Brigades, and *Volks* Rocket Projector Brigades, all of which will be discussed in Section VII.

From the organization point of view, the significance of the *Volks Grenadier* Division lies in its decrease of personnel and increase of small automatic weapons, particularly submachine guns (and the sturmgewehr 'assault rifle'). Also company and battalion trains have been merged into battalion supply platoons, thus freeing the company commander from all duties other than operational and facilitating a more even distribution of all types of supplies with less personnel. Bazookas replace all antitank guns in the infantry regiments; the artillery regiment is organized in batteries of six guns instead of four, with one battalion of eighteen 75-mm guns replacing a normal battalion of twelve 105-mm gun/howitzers. An additional new feature is the formation of a divisional supply regiment which combines all the divisional services except the military police detachment which has been assigned to the division headquarters. This type of division is shown on the Figures 14 and 15 as *Volks Grenadier* Division.

e. *SS* Infantry Division (*SS Grenadierdivisionen*) (Three *SS* Regiments of Two Battalions Each). The great majority of German infantry divisions are army infantry divisions. However, there are also several *SS* infantry divisions (*SS-Grenadierdivisionen*) which have been formed by the armed *SS* (*Waffen-SS*). This type of division is organized similarly to the Infantry Division, 1944 Type, but it has slightly stronger components and includes an organic antiaircraft battalion.

UNIT	Pers	LMGs	Hv MGs	7.92-mm AT Rs	75-mm AT Guns	20-mm AA/AT Guns	50-mm Morts	81-mm Morts	75-mm Inf Hows	150-mm Inf Hows	105-mm Gun/Hows	105-mm Guns	150-mm Hows	Flame Throwers C	Armd Vehicles	Mtrcls	Mtr Vehicles	H-Dr Vehicles	Hs
Div Hq	158	2														17	31		
Rcn Bn	625	25	8		3	3	3	4	2						3	45	30	3	213
Sig Bn	474	17														32	103	7	52
Inf Regt	3,250	123	36	27	12		27	18	6	2						47	73	210	683
Inf Regt	3,250	123	36	27	12		27	18	6	2						47	73	210	683
Inf Regt	3,250	123	36	27	12		27	18	6	2						47	73	210	683
Arty Regt	2,500	32									36	4	8			40	105	229	2,274
AT Bn	550	18			36											45	114		
Engr Bn	843	34		9		8								20		44	87	19	52
Div Serv	2,300	30														88	253	245	735
Total[1]	17,200	527	116	90	75	11	84	58	20	6	36	4	8	20	3	452	942	1,133	5,375

[1] A Repl Bn may be added to any Inf Div.

Figure 8.—Infantry Division, Old Type, total strength 17,200.

Index

Page numbers in *italic* refer to illustrations and captions

UNIFORMEN
DES DEUTSCHEN H

DIENSTGRADABZEICHEN us

SCHULTERKLAPPEN (Unteroffizier- und Mar

Oberwachtmeister
(Oberfähnrich)
Kav.

Feldwebel
(Pi.)

Fähnrich
(Panzerrgt.)

Unter

KRAGENPATTEN MIT GEWEBTEN
LITZEN ZUM WAFFENROCK

Uffz. und Mannschaften
(Kavallerie)

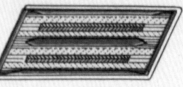

Wehrmachtbeamte ohne Offizierrang

DIENSTSTELLUNGS-ABZEICHEN